The VROOMS of the FOOTHILLS

WHEN THE WORK'S ALL DONE THIS FALL

Titles in the series
The VROOMS of the FOOTHILLS:

The VROOMS of the FOOTHILLS

Volume 3

WHEN THE WORK'S ALL DONE THIS FALL

Bessie Vroom Ellis

TRAFFORD

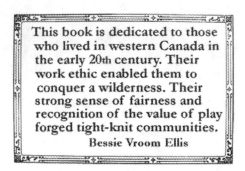

This book is dedicated to those who lived in western Canada in the early 20th century. Their work ethic enabled them to conquer a wilderness. Their strong sense of fairness and recognition of the value of play forged tight-knit communities.

Bessie Vroom Ellis

Order this book online at www.trafford.com
or email orders@trafford.com

Most Trafford titles are also available at major online book retailers.

Front cover: Ina (Logan McWhirter) and Essie Dyer (right), sisters, bringing lunch to threshing crew, circa 1900, courtesy Essie McWhirter Cox
Title page: G.R. "Geordie" Annand, Pass Creek (Blakiston Brook), Waterton Park, 1948, Author's Collection
Back cover: Bessie Vroom, Pincher Creek, AB, 1944, Author's Collection; Hauling boiler for building of Prince of Wales Hotel, Waterton Park, May 29, 1927, Author's Collection
Front and back cover design; editing; photographic restoration and layout: Edi-May Annand Smithies

Printed in the United States of America.

ISBN: 978-1-4269-5626-3 (sc)

Trafford rev. 03/11/2011

 www.trafford.com

North America & International
toll-free: 1 888 232 4444 (USA & Canada)
phone: 250 383 6864 ♦ fax: 812 355 4082

In about 1910, Miss Gertrude Ward and her sister-in-law Mrs. David Ward of Fishburn, AB, collect wild flowers. *Glenbow Archives NA-185-55*

CONTENTS

Acknowledgements

With great gratitude I acknowledge the gracious help and support of those who assisted me in this work, especially my parents Ralph & Mollie Vroom; my children: Edi-May Annand Smithies, my main researcher and editor; Evelyn Annand Lailey, David Annand and Jim Annand, and their spouses; my brother, Donald Vroom and his wife, Doreen Lund Vroom; my sister-in-law Moe Swainger Vroom (Mrs. Bill Vroom); my sister Marion Vroom Grechman; and my good friend Joe Meade for ongoing encouragement and support. I especially thank Shelley McConnell, wife of Jim Annand, for helping by using her expertise in map-making.

I would like to acknowledge the valuable contributions made to this book by many friends and relatives in sharing both their photographs and their memories. If some photos appear less than perfect, it is because the original is small or old. However, many photos are unique and I want to preserve them for future generations. The generosity of the following people has enabled me to write about some of the very interesting history of southwest Alberta history that might otherwise go unrecorded. Specifically, I would like to thank Ken Allred, MLA, Sonia Chiesa Barclay Anderson, George "Geordie" Annand, Alf & Ella Stevenson Baker, Betty Annand Baker, Marguerite Link Bennett, Nieves Primeau Brister, Barbara Baker Brown, Katherine Bruce, Harold and Gada Anderson Bruns, Jean McEwen Burns, Gladys Foster Charman, Alvina Bond Clavel, Barbara Christiansen, Effie Lowry Christiansen, Marie 'Mickey' Christiansen, Hector Cote, Essie McWhirter Cox, Gladys Cummins, Hugh Dempsey, Dr. John Dormaar, Jane-Ellen Doubt, Donna Barclay Elliott, Jim English, Anna de Geest Gladstone, Frank & Linnea Hagglund Goble, Heather Bruce Grace, George & Kay Kettles Hagglund, Bessie Thomas Halton, Elaine Black Hamilton, Trudy Handl, Dave Harder; Mary, Buster, Debbie and Maxine Higbee Haug; Jim Hewitt, Alan Hochstein, Edith "Toots" Jack Hochstein, Lester & Doris Hochstein, J.C. "Jack" Holroyd, Ruby Peters Jaggernath, Alma "Jo" Ballantyne Johnson, Rod & Nancy Kretz, Robin LaGrandeur, Robert Lang, June Perrett Udal Leggott, Kathleen "Kay" McRae Leigh, Bill Link, Gavin MacKay, Joyce McFarland, Doug and Lee Gingras McClelland, Elva Ballantyne McClelland, Frances Riviere McWhirter, Bertie Jenkins Patriquin, Jack & Robina Hewitt Peterson, Olga Zurowski Petrone, Lorraine Riviere Pommier, Brian Prigge, Judy Prince, Anne Russell Raabe, Dr. Brian & Mary Ann Healey Reeves, Ginger Link Reimer, Adeline Cyr Robbins, Charlie Russell, Gordon Russell, Dick Russell, John Russell, Adam 'Dutch' and Hazel Anderson Truitt, George & Shirley Branner Tyson, David and Anna Vroom, Peter Vroom, and Pat Gannon Wellings.

As well, I am grateful to Becky Mitchell-Skinner of Parks Canada, Waterton Lakes National Park; Colleen Bains of the Waterton Natural History Association, Waterton Park; Farley Wuth, Curator, Kootenai Brown Pioneer Village, Pincher Creek; Lindsay Moir, Senior Librarian, Glenbow Museum Library & Archives, Calgary; and Library and Archives Canada, Ottawa, for their very capable research assistance, so willingly given.

If there are other people I have missed with my thanks, I apologize for the omission. Readers who would like to contact me are invited to do so in care of Trafford Publishing.

PROLOGUE

There's an old cowboy song that contains the poignant line: "I'm going to see my mother when the work's all done this fall." In the song, a young cowboy is trail-driving a large herd of Texas longhorns across the Great Plains of North America. They are taking the cattle to one of the many railheads on one of several railway lines running from the west to the Chicago stockyards for marketing in the east.

In the song, during the night a fierce thunder and lightning storm strikes. The herd stampedes. The young cowboy rides his saddle horse at break-neck speed trying to head off the frenzied cattle and get them settled down before they scatter far and wide. Unfortunately, his saddle horse sticks its foot into a badger hole and falls, throwing the young cowboy over its head and onto the hard-packed earth. Without medical aid, he dies. The last words he speaks are, "And I'll not see my mother when the work's all done this fall."

The story told by that song represents the many hardships our forbearers in North America faced and survived while settling this vast land.

The work that people do evolves over the centuries. Methods and machinery also change. Many tasks that people performed during the 20th century do not exist in the 21st century. New methods and new and more powerful machinery have increased peoples' production.

My third book, *The Vrooms of the Foothills, Volume 3: When the Work's All Done this Fall,* contains about 270 pictures showing the many different ways in which people made a living in the late 19th and early to mid 20th centuries. This book also tells of the fun families had at their social events.

These pictures are from the collections of descendants of pioneers and homesteaders in southwestern Alberta. The machinery they are using

Alena Munro Vroom

can be viewed in various museums and pioneer villages across Canada and the US.

Children are a favourite subject for amateur photographers of all ages. The pictures of children that appear in Volume 3 show that children have a strong, inherent urge to play, especially with animals. Children will play with whatever animals are close by. If they have only a cow to ride they will ride the cow.

No matter what animal children are playing with their play patterns are basically the same. Moreover, if children cannot have domesticated animals they will try to catch wild animals and then try to tame them. And, if children do not have store-bought toys, they will make a toy or a game out of whatever scraps of machinery, rope, and so on that they can find around the place.

Mollie Tyson Vroom

I hope that my readers will be as surprised as I was by the number of different ways in which our forbearers made a living for themselves and their families.

I also hope that the pictures in my book, many of which show people operating 20th century machinery, will give a better idea of how work in southwestern Alberta, and in much of western Canada, was done in years gone by.

But, my most enduring wish is that these pictures record how our forbearers and their children enjoyed the simplest of recreational activities.

Chapter 1, **Gifts from the Earth,** tells how homesteaders in western Canada found vast forest lands on the surface of and rich mineral deposits underneath their land. To access their new homes or harvest its forest and mineral wealth people needed a network of communication services. Pictures in Chapter 1 show raw horsepower and manpower, often the only sources of energy available, being used to put this infrastructure in place. The early settlers are also shown relaxing with family and friends.

Ralph Ernst Vroom

Chapter 2, **Ranching, the Real West**, looks at the progression of homesteaders' lives. Often the first buildings that homesteaders built were made of logs. However, as soon as they proved up on their homesteads most homesteaders built a second house and a new barn using sawn lumber.

Homesteaders increased their herds and flocks from year to year, selling surpluses for cash for family needs. Their work focused on securing adequate food, clothing and shelter for their families. Adequate food depended on raising a garden for vegetables and raising their own animals or hunting wild game for meat. This meant feeding and sheltering their animals in spring, summer, fall and winter.

With valiant hearts homesteaders met the challenges and went on to raise families to carry on for succeeding generations. Moreover, they steadfastly worked to provide an element of fun and a sense of belonging for themselves and their neighbours. Photos showing examples of work and recreation of ranchers are featured in Chapter 2.

Chapter 3, **Love Those Animals,** shows the many ways in which the immigrants who settled in southwestern Alberta brought joy into their lives. This chapter emphasizes the part that animals, especially dogs and horses, played in bringing fun into people's daily lives. The early settlers were dependant on animals for travelling from place to place whether to visit a neighbour, who might live a couple of miles away, or to attend church, which might be 10 miles away. Many children rode on horseback to get to school. The whole family worked hard and consequently played hard. Whenever there was a lull in ranch or farm work people took a break from their busy lives. Animals, especially horses of various sizes and breeds, frequently supplied the energy for travelling to community events year round.

Chapter 4, **First We Work,** contains pictures featuring a variety of ways people earned a living in the early to mid-20th century. Once their homesteads were proved up on, and a new house and barn built, some people looked to expand their holdings. Many homesteaders sold their land to a neighbour and went into business in a nearby town. Gradually the number of people in a district decreased and the size of people's land holdings increased. That trend continues into the 21st century.

Even though people worked hard, they did not forget to play. The children's poem *"Twenty Froggies,"* by the English poet George Cooper contains a line saying *"First we work, then we play."* The people of southwestern Alberta went to great pains to ensure that their lives contained a healthy amount of play.

Chapter 5, **It's Off to School We Go!,** showcases photos illustrating that the education of their children was a priority of homesteaders and settlers. They formed independent districts to build schools. Inside the generally rectangular schoolhouses was one large room, where as many as 40 wooden desks accommodated children ranging from 5½ years to 16 or 17 years of age. Some schools had a boys' and a girls' cloakroom.

Some pupils had as far as five miles to go to school. Teachers and pupils walked, rode horseback or drove a horse-drawn cart. A few had a bicycle. Softball was the favourite recess game in spring, summer and fall. Fox and geese and hare-and-hounds were popular winter games. Community and family recreation activities provided weekend fun. If the reader wants more information, *Unfolding the Pages* gives a history of schools in the Pincher Creek area.

Chapter 6, **Fireside Hobbies,** features examples of home crafts that people engaged in, some while living in relative isolation. Hobbies women and girls pursued included: photography, painting in oils and water colours, rag rug-making, knitting, crocheting, and designing and sewing their own and their children's clothes. Boys made model airplanes, even a model farm. Men decorated their leather clothing and made hand-tooled designs on saddles and bridles for their horses. Children made up new games to play and variations of old games. Pictures in Chapter 6 emphasize the creativity and artistic ability of the people of southwestern Alberta.

Chapter 7, **Independent Souls,** talks about the varied businesses founded by people who wanted to do things their own way. It shows women thriving in unexpected situations in which they found themselves. One quarter section of land was not big enough to provide a living for a family and some homesteaders did not want to become farmers or ranchers on a long term basis. Some families really wanted to make their homestead their home, so they bought land from nearby homesteaders. The people who sold their homesteads often went into business in a nearby town. Also, as homesteaders' family members grew in number the older children had to seek a living elsewhere. They, too, sometimes went into business earning a living as best they could.

Chapter 8, **Passions,** has pictures illustrating the various passions that people pursued in the early to mid 1900s. A passion in this context is any long-tem project or ongoing activity in which someone is keenly interested. The project may or may not be financially rewarding, but it is always personally rewarding. Pursuing one's passion makes what might otherwise be a rather humdrum life worthwhile and even exciting.

Chapter 9, **Love Thy Neighbour,** illustrates how communities are held together by various organizations and family activities that take people outside of themselves and their own lives. Pioneer families and homesteaders were sustained to a large extent by the churches of various denominations that they built. They also joined forces to construct other buildings that would benefit the whole community. Various youth groups helped boys and girls living in small, isolated communities to feel proud of their individual and group achievements.

Informal community groups that raised money to help furnish community-built buildings brought the skills of various women to the fore. Special family celebrations brought people together. The generosity and empathy of neighbours in a particularly stressful situation helped to forge friendships that lasted a lifetime. Even wars brought people closer together, as they clung to each other for hope and comfort after receiving a terse note containing the dreaded message that started, "We regret to inform you…"

Elizabeth Mary and George Wilson Tyson

Oscar Vroom

GIFTS FROM THE EARTH

Homesteaders in western Canada found vast forests on the surface and rich mineral deposits under their land. However, people needed a network of services to access their new homes and harvest this forest and mineral wealth. Chapter 1 shows pictures of this infrastructure being put in place when horsepower and manpower were the main sources of energy. Interspersed with pictures of work are photos showing the early settlers relaxing with family and friends.

About 1915, this photo taken looking northwest shows the abandoned tipple for one of the four coal mines operating at Beaver Mines, AB, in the early 1900s. The tipple was at the bottom end of a chute that started at the mouth of a coal mine about half-way up a hill on the west side of Beaver Mines Creek Valley The coal chute crossed over the road that ran south from the village of Beaver Mines at a point less that one-half mile south of the location of the Beaver Mines General Store in 2011. The tipple dumped lignite coal into railroad freight cars standing on the Kootenay & Alberta Railway line. This was a spur line that ran southwest from the main line of the CPR just west of Pincher Station to Beaver Mines. Coal mining in the Beaver Mines area started in 1909 when a 1500 foot tunnel hit a seam of hard lignite coal. Large scale mining in the area ended in 1915 when the coal went soft, turning to bituminous coal. By the 1930s all that was left of some of the mines were holes in the hillsides, the evenly spaced concrete blocks that once supported this tipple, and a concrete pit filled with water located between this tipple and the railroad right-of-way that led to the round house about one-half mile further south. Only Frank Holmes's mine, known locally as Number One coal mine, still operated on the road between the village of Beaver Mines and our ranch. *Courtesy Marguerite Link Bennett*

Located at Mountain Mill on Mill Creek southwest of Pincher Creek, this sawmill is shown in 1886 when it was owned and operated by the Peter McLaren Lumber Co. The mill supplied lumber to build homesteaders' and settlers' homes in the area as early as 1880. The sawmill and stone grist (flour) mill were built by the Dominion Indian Department, which sold the mill and timber limits to Senator Peter McLaren of Ottawa in 1881 (Map 7). The mill pond shown here holds logs cut in Gladstone Valley and floated downstream. In the background are the original McLaren ranch buildings; (left to right) cow barn, horse barn, bunkhouse, McLaren ranch house and blacksmith shop. Later these buildings and the McLaren ranch were bought by Fred and Anne Harley Link, who raised their family here. At the far left is the sawmill. The grist mill is barely visible; a small part of its roof shows at the right end of the sawmill roof. The sawmill and grist mill were run by water-powered turbines. *Glenbow Archives NA-2480-1*

Holger Hagglund, about 1929, is steadied by his dad, Jack (Helga), atop a work horse. To haul logs out of the forest, the horse was hitched to a singletree which was attached to the log using a heavy chain. A worker leads the horses slowly along the skid trail dragging the logs to a nearby sawmill.

Jack Hagglund was the brother of Otto and Erik Hagglund. They emigrated from Sweden in the early 1900s. Otto and Erik both homesteaded in Pleasant Valley, a picturesque east-west valley that joins the north-south Gladstone Valley near the site of the old Gladstone Valley School. Otto, and his wife Carrie, stayed in Pleasant Valley and raised a family there. Erik, his wife, Olga, and their children, Hilding, Linnea and Esther, moved to Waterton Park where they ran tourist businesses until retiring. Hilding married Miss Florence Moss and with her ran Crandall Lodge until his death in 1946. Linnea married Frank Goble and ran Frank's Café in Waterton Park until retiring and moving to Cardston. Esther married George Allred and ran the Waterton Auto Bungalows in Waterton Park for many years, eventually selling it and moving to Pincher Creek where they built and operated the Parkway Motel until retiring. *Courtesy G & K Hagglund*

In 1919, George Baker stands (left) outside the cabin where he stayed while working at Oil City, Waterton Park. In 1902, Oil City was the site of the first producing oil well in western Canada. With him are Norman Connor of Michigan (middle) and Joe Dietrich of Cardston (right). George got his start by working very hard from the time he was young. Born in England in 1902, George came to Canada in 1908 with his mother, Elsie, and sister, Ella (Mrs. Russell Broomfield). George's father, William, had immigrated to Canada in 1907, homesteading in Gladstone Valley, south of our ranch. In 1918, George worked in Turner Valley, coming to Waterton to work with a drilling crew at Oil City in 1919.

In a few years George had saved enough money to buy a Model T truck, establishing the Park Transport Company in 1921. He hauled supplies from Cardston to Waterton Park weekly. Within a few years he extended his route to Lethbridge. George and his wife, Betty (daughter of George and Betsy Annand), carried on their successful businesses in Waterton for more than 40 years. *Courtesy Betty Annand Baker*

Skirting the east side of Bellevue Hill in Waterton Park, these tracks are messengers from the past. They were still readily visible when my daughter and I walked the trail in 2010. Oil Trail was carved more than 100 years ago by heavy freight wagons loaded with boilers and drilling equipment bound for the first oil well in western Canada at Oil City. Nearby, one branch of the Oil Trail headed south toward what became Waterton townsite. The other branch forded Pass Creek just behind the base of the right hill and went on to Oil City along the narrow, treacherous road past Blue (Crandell) Lake and down into Cameron Creek Valley (Map 6). *Courtesy E Smithies*

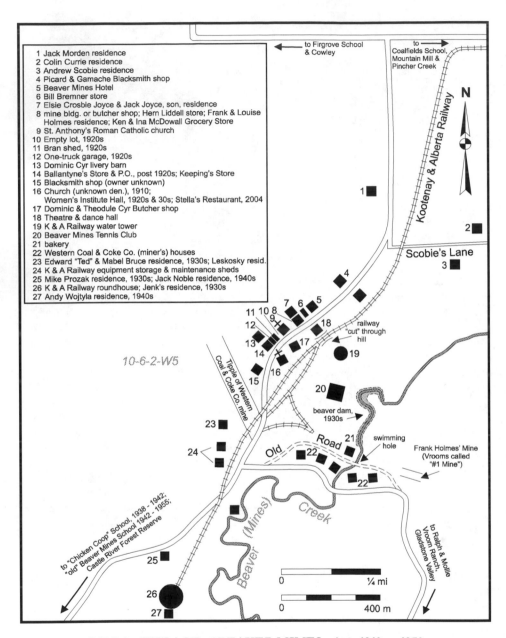

1 Jack Morden residence
2 Colin Currie residence
3 Andrew Scobie residence
4 Picard & Gamache Blacksmith shop
5 Beaver Mines Hotel
6 Bill Bremner store
7 Elsie Crosbie Joyce & Jack Joyce, son, residence
8 mine bldg. or butcher shop; Hern Liddell store; Frank & Louise
   Holmes residence; Ken & Ina McDowall Grocery Store
9 St. Anthony's Roman Catholic church
10 Empty lot, 1920s
11 Bran shed, 1920s
12 One-truck garage, 1920s
13 Dominic Cyr livery barn
14 Ballantyne's Store & P.O., post 1920s; Keeping's Store
15 Blacksmith shop (owner unknown)
16 Church (unknown den.), 1910;
   Women's Institute Hall, 1920s & 30s; Stella's Restaurant, 2004
17 Dominic & Theodule Cyr Butcher shop
18 Theatre & dance hall
19 K & A Railway water tower
20 Beaver Mines Tennis Club
21 bakery
22 Western Coal & Coke Co. (miner's) houses
23 Edward "Ted" & Mabel Bruce residence, 1930s; Leskosky resid.
24 K & A Railway equipment storage & maintenance sheds
25 Mike Prozak residence, 1930s; Jack Noble residence, 1940s
26 K & A Railway roundhouse; Jenk's residence, 1930s
27 Andy Wojtyla residence, 1940s

to Firgrove School & Cowley

to Coalfields School, Mountain Mill & Pincher Creek

Kootenay & Alberta Railway

N

Scobie's Lane

10-6-2-W5

Tipple of Western Coal & Coke Co. mine

railway "cut" through hill

beaver dam, 1930s

Old Road

swimming hole

Frank Holmes' Mine (Vrooms called "#1 Mine")

to "Chicken Coop" School, 1938 - 1942; "old" Beaver Mines School 1942 - 1955; Castle River Forest Reserve

Beaver (Mines) Creek

to Ralph & Mollie Vroom Ranch, Gladstone Valley

0   ¼ mi
0   400 m

MAP 1   VILLAGE of BEAVER MINES, circa 1910 to 1950
In 2011, the village consists of some private residences and a few businesses nestled peacefully against low foothills on the road to West Castle Ski Resort. It is hard to imagine that in the early 1900s Beaver Mines was a bustling coal mining town with as many as 300 miners' families living there. A variety of businesses contributed to the lively life of the community. *Illustration by Edi-May Smithies, Cartography by Shelley McConnell*

Zeke Jones, about 1905, beside his homestead cabin at the mouth of Blind Canyon in the Yarrow Creek district northwest of Twin Butte. Zeke lost a leg in a sawmill accident when he was young, but didn't let that keep him from doing the hard work of a cowboy. Zeke came from Anaconda, MT, with Bill and Dora Gabelhei Terrill in August 1902. He was Bill's stepbrother. They were delivering cattle to H.C. & 'Madam' Glasgow at Twin Butte. Zeke also trapped and hunted coyotes. Here he has one at his feet. These wily scavengers raided the chicken and sheep flocks of southern Alberta homesteaders at every opportunity. Sometimes the task of herding sheep fell to one of the children in a family. Like other homesteaders, Zeke sold the coyote pelts for much-needed cash to make improvements on his homestead. A bachelor for many years, Zeke eventually married a widow, Mrs. Hugh Roberts, and helped raise her two children. *Courtesy E Cox*

Bill Vroom stands with the first elk he shot for food for the family in 1946 at the age of 15 years. Bill shot this elk to the east of Beaver Mines, near our ranch house. He used a horse and singletree to drag the whole animal home. Then Bill and Dad butchered the elk, cut the meat into quarters and stored it in a snow bank to keep the meat fresh. We actually ate very little elk meat fresh. Instead, Mom and Dad canned the meat and kept it until summer time when it became a real delicacy to serve as a treat to unexpected visitors.

To can meat they first cut the meat into serving size pieces. They put the raw meat into clean glass jars, adding a small quantity of salt to heighten the taste. When they got a dozen jars filled they put the jars in the hot water, adding enough more to cover the jars with about an inch of water. Then they added more wood to fire and heated the water in the boiler and kept it at a rounding boil for three hours to ensure that the meat was thoroughly cooked and that any bacteria that might create spoilage was eliminated. They canned one dozen jars of meat a day until it was all canned and stored in the root house. Bill's first success led to his becoming an expert hunter, horseman and outdoorsman. Ultimately Bill had a career of more than 30 years as a National Park warden. During that time he served in several districts in Banff. He helped pioneer the rescue of mountain climbers by dangling on a rope under a helicopter along cliff faces, with the climber pulled up in a basket. *Author's Collection*

Deer and elk were the most common game animals shot in the Gladstone Valley-Beaver Mines area during the 1930s and 1940s. Antelope did not range there. To get a different kind of hunting experience, Dwaine Barclay travelled to the Medicine Hat-Brooks area to shoot antelope.

The Barclays, like other families, preserved some of the delicious meat. To ensure that they had a variety of food for the whole year, homemakers also preserved excess vegetables from their gardens. They also preserved wild fruit, such as strawberries, raspberries, Saskatoon berries, as well as making jams and jellies from various wild and tame fruit. The Angelo and Osanna Chiesa family, who lived on the Castle River, would process up to 30 quarts of food in a day. *Courtesy Sonia Chiesa Anderson*

Gophers were abundant in the 1920s and 30s. In the summer time school children on farms and ranches in Alberta trapped gophers as a pest control project. After killing a gopher the young trapper cut off the animal's tail. The district councillor had authority to pay one cent per tail. A summer's trapping would net a significant amount of cash for an industrious child.

Michael Bruce took this picture at Sarcee Military Camp at Calgary. Michael, his dad and older brother, Ronald, were attending summer militia exercises. They had to supply their own horses and riding equipment. The three Bruce men rode the 120 miles or so to Calgary and home again to Beaver Mines. *Courtesy Katherine Bruce*

Alphie Primeau in 1943 skinning a muskrat that he trapped on one of the lakes on his ranch northwest of Twin Butte as his daughter, Nieves, watches him.

Trapping muskrats was recreation for farmers and ranchers in the area, as well as a way to earn much-needed extra cash. These lithe brown animals frequented the numerous lakes and ponds in southwestern Alberta during the 1920s to the 1940s (Map 2).

Trappers sold muskrat pelts for a good price in the 1930s. The soft brown muskrat fur was a popular trim for women's clothing and accessories. Muskrat pelts were also used by the native Indians for ceremonial robes. The storage shed where Alphie kept his trapping gear is in the background. *Courtesy Nieves Primeau Brister*

This 1928 photo shows an unknown man on horseback with wild animal pelts thrown across his horse. There are coyote skins in front of his saddle and wolf pelts behind. Four coyote hounds stand watching. They are waiting for the hunt to continue. Windmills were used to pump water from deep wells on the prairies. Written on the back: "A successful hunt." *Courtesy Katherine Bruce*

This massive coal-fired engine once operated on the Kootenay & Alberta Railway spur line that ran from the main line of the CPR west of Pincher station to Beaver Mines. The trains ran daily from 1912 until the mines closed in 1915, hauling cars of coal. When the coal turned soft, the trains stopped running. Few reminders of that era remain in the area in 2011. *Courtesy Bill Link*

This remarkable close-up is of the huge wooden railway trestle that spanned Mill Creek Valley at Mountain Mill, circa 1911. The railway right of way at the east end of the trestle shows clearly. The photo is taken looking almost straight east from the west side of the valley. The right of way was built of soil and rock hauled by local men driving mule teams. The Mountain Mill Church built in 1906 is in the right foreground. The dirt road leading to Pincher Creek and making an 'S' curve on the west side of the valley shows in the foreground. (Map 7) *Courtesy Bill Link*

About 1911, a man driving a team of mules works on the railway grade on the east side of Mill Creek Valley before the trestle was built at Mountain Mill. Mules and dump wagons were used to build the grade. When it rained, or after a snow melt, the road up the hill was very slippery. Wide 'S' curves enabled teams pulling heavy loads to climb out of the steep-banked valley. *Glenbow Archives NB-18-4*

For about 30 years Geordie Stewart (right) kept the greens at the Waterton Park golf course in top condition. In 1934, Mr. Stewart hauls water from Pass Creek (Blakiston Brook) to water the greens. The second wooden bridge over Pass Creek, built in 1921, is in the background. The first bridge, built in 1912, was a bit further up stream. In the 1950s the Waterton golf course was upgraded and a sprinkler system was installed. Geordie's wife, Arta Smith Stewart, was from Gladstone Valley and a long time friend of Mom and Dad's. *Courtesy Betty Baker*

This shows the iron bridge across the Highwood River at High River, AB, July 1927. There were no houses along the river then. The water looks near flood stage. When he took this picture, Michael Bruce, along with his father, Edward, and brother, Ronald, were riding their horses to Calgary from Beaver Mines to take summer militia training at Sarcee Camp in Calgary. *Courtesy Katherine Bruce*

Forest rangers and their families lived in isolated cabins hours away from the nearest town. Living conditions were not luxurious. They learned to be self-sufficient. Here in 1929, forest ranger Reginald Prigge re-shingles the roof of Mill Creek Ranger cabin. (Map 3) His daughter, Billie, and son, Brian, are his helpers. *Courtesy Brian Prigge*

About 1955, this fuel truck travelling aboard the barge "Montalta" is taking a load of fuel oil to the US warden station at Goathaunt, MT, at the head of Upper Waterton Lake in Glacier National Park. The barge and the truck were operated by the Park Transport Company, which was owned by George and Betty Annand Baker. *Courtesy Alfred Baker*

A team of buffalo pulls a Red River cart, the cart being a mode of travel in western Canada in the 19th century. The driver is dressed as a frontiersman. His passenger is an army officer. People of varying ages perch on corral railings watching the parade. Local people always made a big effort to put on a good show for the entertainment of visitors to their summer fairs and rodeos. *Courtesy Brian Prigge*

The above pictures show the two boilers that were in the powerhouse of the Prince of Wales Hotel in Waterton Park. They are being hauled during the hotel's construction from the rail head at Hillspring, AB, in May 1927. In the top picture, a boiler is pulled over snow-covered ground by a team of eight horses driven by one man. The second boiler, brought in over muddy roads - a much more difficult task - was pulled by 16 horses in four teams driven by four men (Djuff, 1999). Nine of 16 horses are shown here. All men were very skilful teamsters. *Author's Collection*

As late as the 1940s, wardens in Canada's National Parks used pack horses to haul the lumber to build their cabins in remote areas. Here, in 1942, Reginald Prigge is hauling lumber to build a cabin in Banff National Park. The long pieces of lumber are being carried by two well-trained, dependable pack horses moving in step with one another along a trail. A third pack horse carries supplies. Over a number of years Mr. Prigge hauled lumber to build warden stations at Egypt Lake, Castle Mountain and Tunnel Mountain in Banff. *Courtesy Brian Prigge*

Henri "Frenchy" Riviere's dog team at his Victoria Peak ranch (Map 4) hitched to an umiak in 1921. Frenchy successfully crossed timber wolves and huskies. From this cross-breeding, and using the largest and strongest pups from successive litters, he built up his famous dog team. When fully grown, these dogs could also carry loads of up to 60 pounds each, serving Frenchy as pack dogs in the mountains in the wintertime. *Courtesy Nieves Brister*

Like his father, James Riviere also built up a team of strong sled dogs. Sometimes, just for fun, he drove them around the countryside in the wintertime. He often came as far north as our ranch at Beaver Mines, a distance about 30 miles. *Courtesy Nieves Brister*

This is the Lethbridge Northern Irrigation District float in a local town parade circa 1930. Irrigation projects were started in southern Alberta in the early 1920s. By the 1930s irrigation's potential was fully realized. The farmers from Mountain View west of Cardston to the north end of the Lethbridge district knew that water was all that was needed to turn the rich prairie soil into a vast crop-producing area. The words on their float: "Sunshine. Soil. Water. Wealth." said it all. *Courtesy Ginger Link Reimer*

The United Irrigation Dam was built south of Glenwood, AB, in 1922. I crossed the dam on the Waterton River about 1935 when I was with visiting my grandparents, George and Mary Tyson. In 1995 Geordie Annand said, *"George Sr. delivered milk to the construction crew. Potatoes were worth $1.00 per 100 lbs"*. The Annands had a dairy herd on their farm on the Belly River before moving to Waterton Park. *Courtesy B Baker*

This is a road construction crew working near Mountain View, AB, in 1935. Men driving teams of horses are a large part of the crew. At least six teams can be seen in this picture. As the drivers file past the grader; other crew members heave boulders into the sturdy grain wagon boxes. The drivers haul the rocks away and circle back to join the queue to pick up another load of rocks. *Glenbow NA-2177-1*

This was Main Street, Pincher Creek, AB, in 1908. There are only ten buildings visible. The livery stable is the closest building, on the right hand side.

The line of telephone poles indicates there were telephones in Pincher Creek as early as 1908. In a 1961 interview Robert Lang told me, "In 1902 there were three stores in Pincher Creek. Jim Scofield had a general store…C. Kettles had a store and a butcher shop…Tim Lebel came and went in partnership with C. Kettles to build a stone store." That store still stands in 2011. *Courtesy Bill Link*

RANCHING – THE REAL WEST

Often the first buildings that homesteaders built were made of logs. As soon as they proved up on their homesteads, most homesteaders built a second house and a new barn using finished lumber. Homesteaders increased their herds and flocks from year to year, selling surpluses for cash for family needs. Their work focused on securing adequate food, clothing and shelter for their families.

Adequate food depended on raising a garden for vegetables and raising their own animals or hunting wild game for meat. This meant feeding and sheltering their animals in spring, summer, fall and winter. With valiant hearts, homesteaders met the challenges and went on to raise families to carry on for succeeding generations. They steadfastly worked to provide an element of fun and a sense of belonging for themselves and their neighbours.

Construction of a fine new barn on the homestead of Erik Hagglund, Gladstone Valley (Map 3), is underway in 1921. Brothers Otto (left) and Erik (right) balance fearlessly on the ridgepole of the gambrel roof of the new barn. It replaces the original, small barn that Erik and Otto built on Erik's homestead when Erik homesteaded the land about 1913. Erik's wife, Olga, sits on the barn door sill with her first two children, Esther (left, born 1919) and Linnea (right, born 1917). Olga, widely renowned as a wonderful cook, had probably brought a meal out to the men so that they could eat on the job rather than taking time to go into the house to eat. The large loft will hold many tons of hay to be used to feed livestock over the winter. *Courtesy F&L Goble*

This is Fred Lund's house in 2000. It was the second house built in 1911 on the Hagglund and Lund homesteads by Eric and Fred (Map 3). It was almost the same design as Eric Hagglund's house. Using rollers, this house was moved several times. On the last move George Hagglund moved this family relic closer to the (dirt) road going to his house. My daughter Edi-May and I saw it there in August 2004. Olga Hagglund came to Eric's homestead as a bride when she emigrated from Sweden. When she saw the cottage that Eric had built for them, Olga thought that it "looked like a doll's house." *Courtesy F&L Goble*

Bill and Jane Barclay on their homestead about 1930 (Map 3); Table Mountain looms in the background. The third family to homestead in Gladstone Valley (1905), they raised nine children. His team of draft horses pulled the heavy plough tearing out tree roots left when the dense forest was felled. While the land was being cleared the Barclay family lived in a tent. They were about twelve miles from the post office when it was at Mountain Mill and eight miles from the Beaver Mines Post Office which opened December 15, 1911. The Barclays were among the first children to attend the Gladstone Valley School, which opened in 1912. *Courtesy D Elliott*

This 1920s photo shows George R. Annand on his homestead quarter west of Twin Butte, AB, SE¼-14-4-30-W4th (Map 4). The team of draft horses pulls a sulky plough used to break up the tough grassland, or sod, on the prairies of western Canada. The horses in George's four-horse team were called "Tex", "Flax" (both were sorrels), "Sleepy" and "Bill". Young George Rae Jr. "Geordie" Annand, who liked to walk bare-footed in the cool dark earth turned over by the plough, poses here with his dad. The soil in the Alberta foothills was quite rocky. Rocks were piled in a large heap with the use of a stone boat. Before the invention of sulky ploughs, walking ploughs were used for sod breaking. The sulky plough was a big improvement over the walking plough because the farmer could now sit in a seat holding the reins. He rode on the plough instead of walking behind it. *Courtesy Betty Baker*

During the lull in ranch work just before the start of summer haying season, calves were branded ready to go out to summer pasture.

Here in 1934 in the field east of the ranch house of Ralph and Mollie Vroom (Map 2) three men are on hand for calf branding. Left to right: Chas. "Charlie" Deschamp (standing and holding a branding iron); Ralph Vroom (on the iron grey horse); George Chamberlaine (on the bald faced horse). The branding iron was heated to red hot in a small campfire near the branding site.

Often the cattle of more than one rancher shared the same range. Branding the calves each spring with a distinguishing mark enabled the ranchers to sort out their own cattle. Each spring Dad checked the general health of our horses and branded new spring colts with his XV bar on the right thigh. He halter broke the yearlings and trained the three-year-olds to be reliable saddle horses. *Author's Collection*

In spring 1938, ten-year-old twin brothers Robin and Ramon LaGrandeur ('circled' riders) are helping to trail a herd of cattle from the IV Ranch east of Pincher Creek to a summer range deep in the foothills southwest of Pincher Creek. Their destination was the Castle River Forest Reserve marked by Table Mountain in the background. The Stock Association of Pincher Creek leased the land, which was located 20 miles west of Pincher Creek. Notes at the top of the picture say: "Buckhorn Ranch, Table Mountain (the Pete LaGrandeur family) lived two miles north from 1932-1944."

A number of small herds from various ranches were driven to the reserve in April. In October, November or December, the stock was driven back to the home ranches. The steers fattened up over the summer were sold to meat packers in Lethbridge and Calgary. More information on the cow camp where the Pete LaGrandeur family lived is in my book *The Vrooms of the Foothills, Vol. 1: Adventures of My Childhood.* Photo by Rey Marr. *Courtesy Robin LaGrandeur*

Here in the 1930s Gordon Hamilton is raking hay for Edward and Mabel Bruce when they lived at Beaver Mines (Map 1). He is putting recently mowed hay into windrows. When the whole field is put into windrows, Gordon will drive his team and rake along the windrows making two or three big bunches of hay along each windrow. The bunches are then thrown into a hayrack and hauled to a stack or the ranch barn where it is stored in the hay mow. *Courtesy Katherine Bruce*

In the 1930s, Carrie and Otto Hagglund on the stack of hay, and their sons Harold (left) and George (right) are the haying crew (Map 3). A large two- or three-pronged hay fork was suspended from a metal pulley, which rolled along a rail attached to the ridge pole of the barn. A heavy rope was attached to the doubletrees of the team of horses. When the person in the rack had the fork firmly planted in the hay he called out a signal to the driver of the team. As the team moved ahead the forkful of hay was pulled up to the ridge pole and along the railing. At just the right moment the person in the hayrack pulled a trip rope that released the hay at the far end of the hayloft. *Courtesy George and Kay Hagglund*

George (Edwina) Cummins, father of Gladys, cutting grain circa 1920 on his farm in the Robert Kerr district using a binder. Horse-drawn binders cut the grain, and then gathered it into bundles while tying each bundle with binder twine. The binder spewed out the bundles, or sheaves, at intervals around the field. The sheaves were put into piles called "stooks," a task which often fell to the farmer's wife and/or his children. Depending on the weather, threshing sometimes went on as late as November. *Courtesy Gladys Cummins*

In many families children of various ages made a big contribution to the farm labour force. Children who lived in town often visited uncles and aunts or grandparents who lived on farms or ranches and helped with farm work, especially in the summers.

Here in 1932 Alton "Hoot" Carlson (left) and his sister, Lucille (MacKay) (right) stook grain on the ranch of their uncle Charlie Joyce near Twin Butte. They were the children of Carl and Ada "Cecily" (Joyce) Carlson of Waterton Park. Alton is about four years old and Lucille is about eight. The children are having a hard time trying to stand the heavy sheaves of grain on end to make a neat stook. The rough straw scratches the children's tender arms. Stooking grain is hard work. *Courtesy Gavin MacKay*

About 1915 Jesse Branner stands atop a loaded bundle rack on his homestead east of Ponoka, AB. Jesse was the father of Shirley Branner Tyson, wife of my cousin George.

A bundle rack was an open-sided rack placed on top of a farm wagon chassis. Men driving bundle racks picked up the sheaves to take them to the threshing machine. When the bundle rack was full the teamster drove over to the threshing machine and heaved the bundles into the hopper. *Courtesy George and Shirley Branner Tyson*

Every homestead family had a vegetable garden and a potato patch. Here A.E. Cox ploughs out the potato crop on his ranch near Mountain Mill west of Pincher Creek, AB. Mr. Cox keeps a steady hand on the reins so that his team walks in a straight line. His son, one of his older children, holds the handles of the walking plough making sure that it stays in the ground at the proper depth to dig up the potatoes. Younger children picked up the potatoes in small pails and dumped them into gunny sacks. The gunny sacks were loaded on a stone boat and hauled to the root cellar for winter storage. To plant potatoes a rancher ploughed long furrows in the potato patch. Seed potatoes were placed in every third furrow. Earth from the fourth furrow covered the planted potatoes. *Glenbow Archives NA-2001-14*

George Annand, Sr. heaves sheaves of wheat hauled from his bundle rack into the hopper of a threshing machine in 1918. A second man stands watching him. In this picture George has nearly emptied his load. As more wheat is put through the threshing machine the straw pile (left centre in this picture) grows larger.

Most homesteaders worked off their homesteads for a few months each year to earn extra cash. While the men were away their wives, left on their own, looked after the children and did the farm work at home.

George took his four-horse team ("Tex", "Flax", "Sleepy and "Bill") and his hayrack/bundle rack to the Kenley Ranch near Magrath, AB, to earn some extra money while proving up on his own homestead. During the summers of 1916-1919, Betsy and Betty (born 1908) were left alone on their homestead west of Twin Butte to look after Geordie (born 1915), the vegetable garden and the dairy cattle. *Courtesy Betty Annand Baker*

Joe Clavel was another Pincher Creek area homesteader who took a team of horses and his hay/bundle rack further out on the prairies to earn cash to provide necessities for his family on his homestead.

Here in the summer of 1926, Joe sits atop his loaded bundle rack watching carefully as a farmer near Ensign, AB, shows off his newest piece of modern equipment - a steam operated tractor. The steam tractor drives the heavy belt that runs the threshing machine. *Courtesy Alvina Bond Clavel*

Wood fires were used for both heating and cooking in homes in the early days in the west. This is the stack of poles that Alphie and Alice Riviere Primeau cut and stacked beside their house southwest of Twin Butte in the fall of 1938 (Map 4). Every day several pieces were cut off a pole and chopped into the right size to fit into the cook stove and heater. Generally children packed in armloads of chopped wood each evening ready for use as the next day's fuel. *Courtesy Nieves Brister*

In about 1940, Alphie and Alice Riviere Primeau's Hereford cattle huddle together to withstand the shock of a September snowstorm. Many worse storms will follow during the winter, but a Chinook will melt the snow so that the cattle can feed outdoors all winter. The soft late afternoon light brightens up the snow-covered Rocky Mountains in the background. *Courtesy Nieves Primeau Brister*

A dry, warm barn was needed to house work horses and saddle horses that were used during all seasons. This 1970 picture shows the *circa* 1930 barn of Henri "Frenchy" and Nellie Gladstone Riviere still standing on their Victoria Peak ranch (Map 4). Inside were several stalls where horses were tied to mangers and some stanchions for milk cows. *Courtesy Nieves Primeau Brister*

Early snowplows didn't get rid of the snow; piles just got higher. The passage between snow mounds became narrower. Often the snow turned to piles of ice following a Chinook. In the 1920s, a man driving a rudimentary snowplow widens a pass between icy heaps in Waterton Park townsite. *Courtesy Betty Baker*

Grizzly bears constantly threatened the livestock of ranchers who lived near the Castle River Forest Reserve. Ranchers could get a permit to kill the bears. Here Charlie Barclay poses with a grizzly he killed in about 1950. *Courtesy Sonia Chiesa Anderson*

This is the cow camp in the Castle River Forest Reserve as Ramón and Robin (twins), and Mary and Esther LaGrandeur, children of Pete and Edith Vliet LaGrandeur, knew it. Grizzly bears that regularly killed cattle were trapped and shot. Inscription reads: "*Bears were hung on pole between the two trees on the right to be skinned. What a beautiful spot. Saw a cougar just to the right, at the spring, while sitting on the front porch with Bear Grease John (Steibertz).*" *Courtesy Robin LaGrandeur*

Southwest Alberta was originally cowboy country. Families who homesteaded and settled there never ceased to enjoy seeing cowboys showing off their skills at local exhibitions and rodeos. Here Mike Yagos, a cowboy/rancher from near Cowley, is riding "Sweetheart" at the Pincher Creek Fair and Rodeo in August 1944. Mike was one of my Dad's long-time friends. *Author's Collection*

In this undated picture, Pete LaGrandeur holds the flag in the air as he judges a calf roping contest. A contestant chases a calf on horseback, ropes the calf and throws it to the ground. When the contestant stands up with his hands in the air, signaling he has finished tying the calf securely, the contest judge drops the flag. The contestant with the fastest time in this exciting event wins. Pete was also one of my Dad's long-time friends. *Courtesy Robin LaGrandeur*

Local fairs and rodeos gave ranch crews, including the chuck wagon drivers, a chance to show off how well they could do their jobs.

Here chuck wagon outfits from various ranches in the Pincher Creek district drive up to the starting line at the Castle River Stampede ready to race with each other. Outriders accompanied the chuck wagons. *Courtesy Katherine Bruce*

It's not easy staying atop a writhing, twisting steer for the required number of seconds. Here a cowboy rides an angry steer at the Pincher Creek Fair and Rodeo in 1944. The rider holds onto a surcingle. A rope is tightened around the steer's flanks to make him buck more energetically. Youngsters start out riding calves at home until they can ride steers in competition at local rodeos. *Author's Collection*

This postcard belonged to my parents, Ralph and Mollie Vroom. Texas cowboy Alf Vivian finishes roping and tying a steer at the Calgary Exhibition and Stampede in 1912. His well trained saddle horse stands holding the lariat taut while Vivian wraps a short rope around the steer's hooves to keep the steer lying on his side. Inscription: *"'Steer roping' at the 'Stampede' 1912, Calgary, Alta. Can. Photo #33 by Marcell". Author's Collection*

LOVE THOSE ANIMALS

There were many ways immigrants who settled in southwestern Alberta brought joy into their lives. This chapter emphasizes the part that animals, especially dogs and horses, played in bringing fun into people's daily lives. The early settlers were dependent on animals for travelling from place to place whether to visit a neighbour, who might live a couple of miles away, or to attend church, which might be 10 miles away. Many children rode on horseback to get to school. Whenever there was a lull in ranch or farm work, people took a break from their busy lives. Horses of various breeds supplied the energy for travelling to community events.

In 1921, when Ralph and Mollie Vroom were first married and living at Mountain Mill (Map 7), Ralph owned two dogs, a blue-grey Border collie, "Tippy" and a light tan Airedale, shown here. Ralph, who had great patience when training an unbroken horse or a puppy, taught the Airedale to ride a horse bareback. When I was about 10 years old and on our ranch at Beaver Mines, I taught my dog "Tippy" to catch any goat I wanted to play with. The goats learned, too. They would run right up to me whenever I called, "Here, Tippy! Here, Tippy!" Photo by Mabel Bruce. *Courtesy Katherine Bruce*

While Col. James Macleod was assistant commissioner for the North West Mounted Police, the family spent the summers of 1890-1893 camping in Waterton Park. Assisted by Kootenai Brown (right), the family sits in a rowboat ready to shove off for a pleasant summer day's outing on Aldridge Bay, Middle Waterton Lake, near Lake Linnet. The Macleod family travelled by team and wagon to Waterton. The Prince of Wales Hotel was built in 1927 on the hill in the background. *Glenbow Archives NA-917-8*

This 1935 picture, taken from atop Crandell Mtn., shows the Scotty Morris house (second from left on main entry road) standing across from Middle Waterton Lake. In August 1938, my Dad, Ralph Vroom, my brother Don, Eileen Lunn, Blanche Pope and I (11 years old) travelled for 10 days by pack and saddle horses from our ranch at Beaver Mines up the Castle River, over the Castle River Divide, and down Blakiston Valley to the Waterton townsite (Map 2) We returned home on a trail that skirted the east side of the mountains. It was a very exciting and memorable trip for me as I loved trail riding, camping, and just riding my favourite horse. *Courtesy F&L Goble*

In the summer of 1941, the Wesley brothers, farmers from Granum, AB, are ready for a day-long ride and fishing trip to Lone Lake in Waterton Lakes Park. The Wesleys rented saddle horses from the Ralph Vroom family at Red Rock Canyon. Going on a fishing trip in the mountains was the Wesleys' reward to themselves for successfully completing the spring and early summer work on their farm. My brother, Don, second from right, was the guide for the trip. Chief Warden, J.C. "Bo" Holroyd determined the qualifications required to be a Park Guide. Although Don was qualified when he was 15, "Bo" wouldn't recommend to Supt. Atkinson that Don get his license until he turned 16 years in August 1940. Don was the youngest person ever to get a Park Guide's license. *Author's Collection*

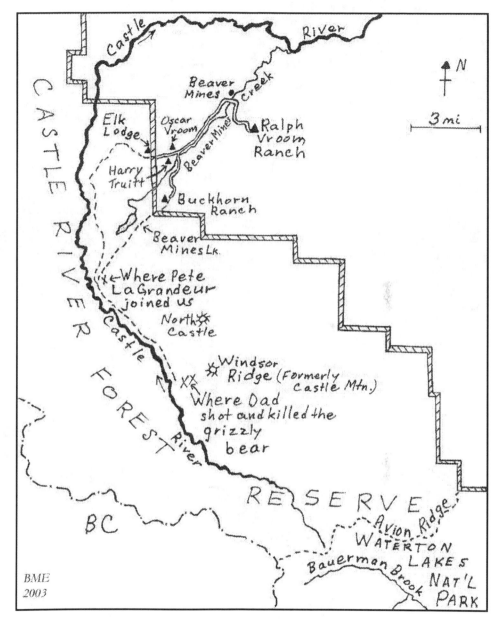

MAP 2 RALPH VROOM RANCH to WATERTON PARK

In August 1938, my Dad, my brother Don, Eileen Lunn, Blanche Pope and I travelled by pack and saddle horses from our ranch at Beaver Mines up the Castle River and down Blakiston Valley to the Waterton townsite. This map is from my first book *The Vrooms of the Foothills: Adventures of My Childhood*. The exciting story of me accompanying my Dad to kill a grizzly bear is told in that book. *Map hand drawn by the Author*

In the 1930s, fishing in the lakes, and rivers of southwest Alberta was a favorite pastime. Visitors were often taken by saddle horse to a fishing hole of a local resident. In the case of old timer Albert Link, standing at left, his favourite hole was almost in his back yard. Albert and a friend share a proud moment as they heft a huge bull trout caught in nearby Mill Creek (Map 7). *Courtesy M Link Bennett*

Billy McEwen was another old-time cowboy. In his younger days he worked for some of the big cattle ranches in southwestern Alberta, such as the Walrond Ranch. When the country opened up for tourists who wanted to see the back country, Billy guided fishing parties to the high mountain lakes in Banff and Waterton Lakes National Parks.

When this late 1930s picture was taken, Billy worked for Morris Bros. Guides & Outfitters in Waterton Park. Here he holds evidence of his prowess as a fisherman - a string of large whitefish that he caught in the fast-flowing waters of the Waterton River at Marquis Hole, which was in an area known as "down behind the hay sheds." *Author's Collection*

Many ranchers in the southwest corner of Alberta took family and friends on fishing and sightseeing trips in the mountains simply for relaxation. They rode gentle saddle horses and carried their bedding, food and cooking equipment on pack horses. Dad made extra money for his ranching operation by taking paying customers on extended outings in the mountains. Here in the late 1930s, Ralph is ready to mount his horse to meet his clients at the entrance to the Castle River Forest Reserve to take them on a fishing trip up the south fork of the Castle River. My Dad, Ralph, and Bert Riggall, were only 2 of 3 outfitters to hold a First Class Alberta Guide License after WWII. *Author's Collection*

John McCrae's graphic poem "In Flanders Fields" comes to mind with this picture. Entitled "A few boys from Cowley," these young men enrolled in the 23rd Alberta Rangers. They are at Sarcee Army Camp, Calgary, July 1916. Most were homesteaders' sons. Many went overseas in WWI. Some of them did not come home. Their mothers and families grieved for them for the rest of their lives. War is so useless! Ralph Vroom, with his hat set at a rakish angle, is second from right, back row. His brother Alfred is in the front row, seated in the middle. *Glenbow Archives NA-5483-15*

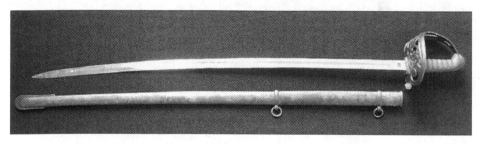

This 23rd Albert Rangers sword and scabbard was one of the few mementoes my Dad, Ralph Vroom, brought home from overseas after WWII. The engraved handle indicates that the sword may have belonged to an officer. *Author's Collection*

As a rule, the men who joined the Cavalry during WWI were already experienced riders. Nevertheless, they all received further training at Sarcee Camp, Calgary. As part of their training in horsemanship, men in the 23rd Alberta Rangers engaged in athletics on horseback. In this 1915 picture, these two soldiers are bareback wrestling. The man on the horse's neck was the winner that day. He stuck on while his opponent fell off. *Courtesy Katherine Bruce*

When Edward Bruce lived at Beaver Mines in the 1930s, he spent six weeks every summer attending militia training at Sarcee Army Camp near Calgary. For him, this was a 'vacation'. Here Edward (left) sits astride "King Cole", while his son Ronald, rides "Battleaxe," his mother's favourite saddle horse. They are ready to ride to Calgary, a trip of over 100 miles. Men attending training at Sarcee were obliged to bring their own horses. New uniforms were not supplied so the militiamen wore old WWI uniforms while at Sarcee. *Courtesy Katherine Bruce*

Here I am at age seventeen leading the 1944 Pincher Creek and District Fair and Rodeo parade. I'm riding a beautiful sorrel horse with white markings and adorned with a simple studded martingale.

I felt greatly honoured as my mount, followed by a marching band, walked smartly along Main Street, head up and ears pointed. It was as if he knew that he was being admired by hundreds of onlookers. He was the favourite saddle horse of his owner, George Sheline, a good friend of my Dad, Ralph. George was rodeo manager that year. *Author's Collection*

Every summer in small and large towns, fairs were held where farmers and ranchers showed off their beloved animals and their riding prowess. Various people judged the entries and chose winners in a number of categories. Standing left to right are H.H. Bossenberry and C.C. Colpman, two local businessmen, and Ralph Vroom, recently returned from overseas with the Royal Canadian Artillery. They are judging entrants in the 1945 parade that signaled the opening of the Pincher Creek Fair and Rodeo. In the background is local rancher, Ken Hassett, leaning forward in his saddle to watch the judges. *Author's Collection*

The most colourful participants of any rodeo parade come from nearby Indian reserves. Here Blackfoot chiefs from the Peigan Reserve at Brocket, dressed in full ceremonial regalia, ride in the 1944 Pincher Creek and District Fair and Rodeo parade. When I was a child, Peigan Indians from Brocket camped at the Castle River Stampede grounds for three days so they could participate in that parade. *Author's Collection*

Waterton Park business people and residents put on a show for park visitors by staging Waterton Days, a festive weekend featuring various events. One event was the opening parade. Riders from around the countryside came into the Park to take part. My sister, Marion Vroom, and her dad, Ralph, are sitting astride their saddle horses beside the home of myself and my husband, Geordie Annand, below Park headquarters on Middle Waterton Lake. They're ready to ride in the parade in July 1952. They rode about 30 miles from our home ranch south of Beaver Mines to get to Waterton Park for this parade. *Courtesy Don Vroom*

End of school picnics were a special treat for students and parents alike. The Waterton Park School Junior Room attends their picnic at the lower camp kitchen, Red Rock Canyon, in June 1948. Back (4th) row, standing: Bob Ayris, Unknown, Betty Underwood, Unknown, Vera Bell Webb, Shirley Stevenson, Nan Delaney, Charles "Chuck" Underwood. 3rd row, standing left: Olga Lund (Mrs. Erik) Hagglund talking to grandson Kenny Allred. 3rd row sitting: David Goble, Jimmy Webb, Gary Webb. 2nd row, sitting: Brian Reeves, Rae Baker, Unknown, Helen Leavitt. 1st row, sitting: Shirley Albiston, Valerie Ayris, Elaine Black (feeding Unknown), Susan Going, Judy Going. I was the Junior Room teacher for 1947-1948. *Author's Collection*

A joy of homemaking in the early 1900s was learning about and enjoying a variety of wild flowers. There were 100s of different flowers growing in fields. People had only to ride out into nearby pastures to pick handfuls of brightly-coloured flowers. In about 1910, Miss Gertrude Ward and her sister-in-law Mrs. David Ward of Fishburn, AB, collect wild flowers. *Glenbow Archives NA-185-55*

In late winter elk, deer and moose shed their old antlers and grow new ones. The older the animal, the more "points" and the larger the antlers it has. Here in 1946, Geordie Annand, of Waterton Park , holds up a large rack of antlers that he found while hiking up the North Fork of the Belly River in the Park with his friend, Jack Christiansen. This animal probably died, or was killed by predators, during the previous winter. Porcupines soon chew up antlers that deer and elk have shed. *Author's collection*

Tourists in Waterton Park often went horseback riding. Here in August 1928, several novice riders sit atop horses from the Henri "Frenchy" Riviere hitching rack located at the forks of Pass Creek. The "dudes" are on the north side of the Prince of Wales Hotel above Lake Linnet. In the background are Crandell Mountain and the tourist horse pasture. That summer the noted New York painter, Winold Reiss, was commissioned by Louis Hill of Great Northern Railway, owner of the hotel, to paint an oil painting of Frenchy. *Courtesy Nieves Primeau Brister*

In 1963 I rode up Hell Roaring Canyon in Waterton Park. On this trail, nearing Crypt Lake, riders must dismount and hike the rest of the way to the lake. The trail follows switchbacks up a mountainside, traverses a narrow ledge with a 1500-foot drop-off, and passes through a tunnel where hikers sometimes have to crawl to get through the narrow space. It emerges onto a grassy meadow and passes over a small ridge for a stunning view of the hiker's goal - Crypt Lake. *Author's Collection*

Dwayne Barclay (left) and his dad, Charlie, pose on their nearly matching saddle horses, "Nellie" and "Lightning," on a warm sunny afternoon. The names people choose for their favourite mounts sometimes reflect the nature of the horse; sometimes people just like a name. "Nellie" was given to Dwaine by the owner of the Buckhorn Ranch so that he could ride to Gladstone Valley School, the same school that his dad, uncles and aunts attended years before. Massive Table Mountain stands silently in the background. *Courtesy Sonia Chiesa Barclay Anderson*

As a teenager, Olga Zurowski worked hard on her father's farm east of Beaver Mines to earn $100 so she could purchase "Swift" from my Dad. In 1939, at 18 years old, she is on "Swift". Olga said, "She was such a beautiful, fast horse; I loved her. Her mane and tail never needed pulling or cutting, just brushing. She was a velvety brown and so intelligent." Olga rode Swift chasing cattle when needed and just for her own pleasure other times. *Courtesy Olga Zurowski Petrone*

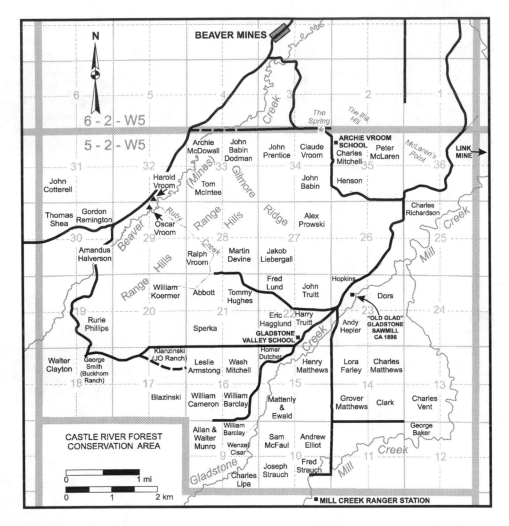

MAP 3 HOMESTEADS IN BEAVER (MINES) CREEK VALLEY and GLADSTONE VALLEY, circa 1910

By 1904 settlers had homesteaded on most of the good land in the bottom of the Gladstone and Beaver Mines Creek Valleys. These are the quarter sections located in Township 5 on which settlers had filed for homestead rights about 1910. Grandpa Oscar Vroom developed his homestead as a working ranch. When Oscar grew elderly, he turned his homestead over to his oldest son, Harold, whose own homestead abutted his father's land. The Archie Vroom School was built by Oscar's brother, Archie, on the homestead of Charles and Mary Ellen "Sis" Buchanan Mitchell. This became our home place when Dad and Mom, Ralph and Mollie Vroom, bought it from Charlie in 1926. Gladstone Valley School and Mill Creek Ranger Station are also shown. Based on information from the National Archives of Canada, Western Canada Land Grants Website. *Illustration by Edi-May Smithies, Cartography by Shelley McConnell*

By early spring, the deer that spend the winter mooching handouts from residents in Waterton Park are quite thin. In 1955, Jean (Bert) Murray is feeding two deer outside her home, the 'old Kootenai Brown' house, just across the highway from Lake Linnet. The Murrays were Geordie's and my next door neighbours. Bert was government storekeeper in the 1950s. Hungry deer sometime came right into our back porch looking for handouts. *Courtesy Barbara & Effie Lowry Christiansen*

John Peerch was a friendly, nature-loving bachelor who, in the 1920s and 30s, lived on Screwdriver Creek a couple of valleys west of my Dad's ranch at Beaver Mines. John found these three as newborn fawns abandoned by their mother. They wore bells, like the deer on the right, so everyone knew they were John's pets. Their antlers are "in the velvet," in this late-winter, 1933 picture. *Courtesy Katherine Bruce*

When the Edward and Mabel Bruce family lived at Beaver Mines, Michael took advantage of the opportunity to observe nature and to take many photographs of what he saw. In April 1928, Michael's brother Ronald, at left, and his father are holding a golden eagle as they stretch its wings out to their full length to show its huge size. Michael's brother, Anthony wrote, "We climbed Table Mountain and what a view there was from the top! The golden eagles were flying all around us and what magnificent birds they were. I am quite sure that the largest of them would have had a wing-span of close to 11 feet and could likely have packed up and carried away a new born fawn or lamb. We were far above the timber line, but on looking down towards the northeast, there was Beaver Lake." *Courtesy Katherine Bruce*

Frances Riviere (Bill McWhirter) hugs her beloved wolf-Husky, "Boy", in 1923. They are in front of her parent's (Frenchy and Nellie Gladstone Riviere) Victoria Peak ranch house (the house is out of view to the right). Victoria Peak is out of view on the left (Map 4). The mountain behind her is where Frances saw her first elk in 1936. As a teen, Frances learned to shoot a rifle and killed elk for meat for the family. Frances' favourite pony as a child was "Bluebeans," a blue-roan appaloosa with white spots on his rump. *Courtesy Frances Riviere McWhirter*

From about 1905 to the early 1960s, one-room country schools dotted the landscape of the Prairie Provinces. In September 1924, Geordie Annand is 8 years old. His hair neatly slicked down and a freshly washed saddle blanket on his horse, he is ready to ride to Mountain View, AB, where he boarded for Grade 1. The next year, Geordie started Grade 3 at Waterton Park School, where he was in the first class to attend the new one-room school. *Courtesy Betty Annand Baker*

Sometimes for a lark people rode a cow. At Mountain Mill about 1915, Bill Doubt has saddled up a very tame cow. Bill was the son of Fred and Isabella Doubt who homesteaded west of Mountain Mill. Bill might have been employed at William Dobbie's sawmill, where his dad managed the lumber yard. The buildings look like those of the (Senator Peter) McLaren ranch at Mountain Mill, later owned by Fred and Ann Harley Link (Map 7). *Courtesy JE Doubt*

FIRST WE WORK

Pictures of the variety of ways in which people earned a living in the early to mid-20th century are highlighted in this chapter. After their homesteads were proved up, many people sold their land to a neighbour and went into business in a nearby town. Gradually the number of people in a district decreased and the size of people's land holdings increased. Even though people worked hard, they did not forget to play. The children's poem, *"Twenty Froggies,"* by the English poet George Cooper contains a line saying *"First we work, then we play."* The people of southwestern Alberta went to great pains to ensure that their lives contained a healthy amount of play.

In 1923 Alphie Primeau with two black bears chained in an old gravel pit. His father-in-law, Henri "Frenchy" Riviere, tamed the young bears and trained them to do tricks so they could perform in Hollywood movies with his huskies. Frenchy brought the bears and huskies back to Canada from Los Angeles to his Victoria Peak ranch (Map 4). *Courtesy N. Primeau Brister*

Here in 1924 Alphie Primeau shows off the tricks of the two black bears. "Ginger" (light-coloured with a broad, dark streak down his back) stands on a box and eats food out of a dish that Alphie holds up to his mouth. In the meantime, "Cinnamon" (dark-coloured) licks the last few morsels of food off a dish that Alphie holds in his other hand. After their return from Los Angeles, Alphie looked after them for a time. *Courtesy Nieves Primeau Brister*

The silent movie "Eternal Love" starring the famous John Barrymore, Sr. and Camilla Horn may have been filmed as early as 1922 in the mountains near Lake Louise in Banff National Park. The movie, which was set in the Swiss Alps, told a forlorn love story.

Experienced mountain guides were needed to carry the filming equipment and the movie stars, using saddle and pack horses, up to the lofty filming sites. Some of those guides were old time cowboys Ira Lum (left) and my Dad, Ralph Vroom (centre), sit sharing their adventure stories with John Barrymore, Sr. (right). Ira was an uncle of Jacqueline Rusch Vroom, my brother Don's first wife. The square flat sheet behind Ira is a scrim, a device used to reflect light onto actors' faces to reduce shadows. The inscription on the photo says *"To Ira best regards John Barrymore". Courtesy Don Vroom and Doreen Lund*

Adventure films involving wild animals appealed to the silent movie audiences of the 1920s. A need developed for tamed wild animals to act in these movies. As well as taking trained black bears to Los Angeles to work in the film *White Fang*, Frenchy Riviere took this tamed timber wolf. "Lady Silver" took the role of the female wolf, 'Lady Jule'. She is seen here lying on stone steps in her enclosure on Frenchy's Victoria Peak ranch in 1926 (Map 4). *Courtesy Nieves Primeau Brister*

George Rae Annand Jr., RCAF, fondly called "Geordie" by his family and friends, stands with his two nephews Rae (left) and Alfred (right). Geordie is on leave visiting his parents, George and Betsy Annand prior to going overseas in 1942. The boys are dressed in child-size air force uniforms. Rae holds a model airplane. The boys are the sons of Geordie's sister and brother-in-law, George and Betty Annand Baker. They are in front of the Baker home in Waterton Park on Evergreen Ave.

Like thousands of other Canadians, a number of young people born and raised in the Waterton area joined the armed services during WWII. Geordie was a flight engineer on many bombing missions before being shot down in 1943 over Mannheim, Germany. He was incarcerated in various German concentration camps until May 1945. *Courtesy Alfred Baker*

Here in 1942, long-time friends and Waterton Park residents, Geordie Annand, RCAF, and Bert Pittaway, Royal Canadian Highlanders, pose for a studio photograph before going overseas. By this time, Geordie has qualified for his engineer's wings. *Author's Collection*

In Trenton, ON, just before going overseas in 1942, Geordie Annand, RCAF, is ready for the worst. He's wearing his flying gear complete with parachute.

Geordie became a member of the exclusive "Silk Worm Club" when his life was saved by his parachute (made of silk in WWII) after being shot down over Germany. Out of a crew of ten, only the pilot and Geordie escaped with their lives. *Courtesy Alf Baker*

Not too many careers were open to women before WWII. Boarding high school students from rural areas was one way women earned extra money. Here Nora Mansfield of the Fishburn, AB, district poses on the verandah of Mrs. Phil Grey's boarding house in Pincher Creek. Fellow high school boarder, Jo Ballantyne of Beaver Mines, snapped this in June 1934. *Courtesy Jo Ballantyne Johnson*

Wardens play a big part in the smooth running of Canada's national parks. In 1933 (left to right) are Jack Giddie, Waterton River district warden; J.C. 'Bo' Holroyd, Supervising Warden stationed at Cedar Cabin on Knight's Lake; Lester S."Mac" McAllister, Pass Creek district warden; Bert Barnes, Belly River district warden. *Courtesy E Hamilton*

A few years after this 1937 photo, Geordie Annand (left) and Bert Pittaway (right) of Waterton Park were both serving overseas with the Canadian Armed Forces. Geordie became an RCAF flight engineer and Bert was with the Royal Canadian Highlanders.

They are doing one of the few jobs available to young men in the so-called "Dirty 30s", working as camp cooks at Tent Camp 1 on the Maskinonge during the building of the Chief Mountain Highway. Camp 1 was located on the old site of Waterton Mills, near the east side of the Waterton River Bridge, on Maskinonge Lake (Map 6). In 2011 it is a picnic site. Photo by Frank Goble. *Courtesy F&L Hagglund Goble*

Ron MacNeill typing a weather report while on duty at the Department of Transport airport at Cowley, AB, in spring 1944. Ron's reports were an essential part of the war effort and classified as confidential. He owned a car and so contributed considerably to the social life of girls in Pincher Creek. Brothers chaperoning their sisters were welcome to ride in the rumble seat. *Author's Collection*

When Dad and Mom, along with Bill and Marion, moved back to the ranch after WWII, Dad started raising pinto Shetland ponies. Bill and Marion gentled the ponies for youngsters to ride safely. About 1950, Bill is holding a Shetland colt, his lariat is on the ground, and some of dad's herd behind. A snubbing post to hold broncs unaccustomed to handling is left of centre in the corral. *Courtesy Donald Vroom*

This is the cook house, about 1928, which was the first building on the Buckhorn Ranch, a well known guest ranch in southwestern Alberta (Map 3). Its large ranch style main house was constructed of upright peeled knotty pine logs. This building had many bedrooms and a large common room, which was used for a dining room or a dance hall.

The first managers of the Buckhorn were Carl and Myrtle Smith. Carl was the son of George Smith, one of the earliest homesteaders in the Beaver Mines Creek Valley. In later years, the ranch was owned by Cliff Cross of Calgary. Cabins were built and a good-sized recreation hall was constructed. A dance every Saturday night attracted people from the entire Beaver Mines-Gladstone Valley area. Music was supplied by a local orchestra consisting of musicians such as Michael Bruce, mandolin; John Babin, violin; Harry Gresl, piano accordion and/or Ruth Tench, piano. Gymkhanas were held on Sundays in the summer time. Riders from throughout the Beaver Mines-Gladstone Valley district rode over to take part in the friendly competitions. *Courtesy Jo Ballantyne Johnson*

The guest lodge, on the hill above the main ranch house, was the social center of the Buckhorn Ranch circa 1950. Dances, and evenings of cards and movies, were held there for the entertainment of the guests. In the mid-morning, many of the guests and ranch hands gathered at the breakfast bar for coffee. *Courtesy Ruby Peters Jaggernath*

This RCAF Supermarine Stranraer Flying Boat was one of 15 seaplanes ferried through Waterton Park in October 1941 It's moored on Knight's Lake in front of Cedar cabin warden station (Map 6).

The planes were flown from the east coast to the west coast to be used for anti-submarine patrol out of Ucluelet, BC. Airmen billeted with Waterton families. Parties and dances were held for their entertainment by the community. *Courtesy Gavin MacKay*

In the summer of 1935 a forest fire, battled by hundreds of men, threatened the town site of Waterton. Taken from the roof of the dance hall, this shows smoke billowing from the blaze about 5 miles away. Residents were on evacuation alert. A sudden shift in the wind blew the fire back on itself. *Courtesy Alf Baker*

Dr. M.J. Brayton's Chevrolet coupe, May 1, 1935. The local small town doctor played a crucial role in the community. The doctor travelled over ungravelled country roads to reach patients. A reliable car was a necessity. Dr. Brayton's handsome son, Darryl, livened up the social life of Pincher

Creek High School students. *Courtesy Gladys Cummins*

1910, J.G. "Kootenai" Brown on Pass Creek flats, Waterton Park. A pioneer homesteader on the the Dardenelles (Map 6) of the Waterton River, he was a strong advocate for establishing the Park. In 1901, he was the first Fishery Officer to guard against poaching. He retired in 1914. Photo by Annie Hescott Jack. *Courtesy E Hochstein*

This log cabin, located on the Kootenai (Waterton) River, was owned by William Callahan who raised remounts for the NWMP. Siblings Tilley and Charlie Puize lived in it before it was moved to Ken McFarland's place in 1964 when the Waterton dam was built. Ken donated it to the Kootenai Brown Pioneer Village. *Courtesy J McFarland*

A Sunday gathering at John and Melcina Truitt homestead, Gladstone Valley, in 1916 (Map 3). Everyone was always made welcome at the Truitts' home. (Left to right) Back row: Gunnar Lund, Washington Mitchell, Erik Hagglund, Fred Gavalin, Lawrence Truitt, Dewey Truitt, Swan Hagglund, "Doc" Truitt, Fred Lund, Alex Barclay.
Front row: Iona Truitt, Olga Hagglund holding Hilding Hagglund, Aggie Barclay, Bessie Truitt, Minnie Barclay, Nellie Barclay, Anna Lund holding Indgred Lund, Mrs. Melcina Truitt holding Adam "Dutch" Truitt. *Courtesy F&L Hagglund Goble*

Waterton Lakes Cafe

CONTINUOUS SERVICE

Bakery, Ice Cream, Confectionery, Tobacco

Lunches for Fishing Parties· Picnics, etc., a Specialty.

MRS. W. A. NIXON, PROP.

The Waterton Lakes Café, sometimes called Nixon's Café, was one of the earliest cafes in Waterton Park townsite. Owned and operated by Florence (Mrs. W. A. Nixon), it was established in the early 1920s. Another ad, which appeared in a 1923 issue of *The Lethbridge Herald*, described the Waterton Lakes Café as being "right opposite the Pavilion". An advertisement for the Tourist Café also was posted in the 1923 issue of *The Lethbridge Herald*. *Courtesy Betty Annand Baker*

1948, Geordie Annand, auto mechanic for the Department of Natural Resources, Waterton Park, rests his arm lightly on a truck beside the old government garage. This garage was replaced in 1960. The replacement resulted in better, healthier working conditions for the garage mechanics. Geordie worked for the Government for 25 years. *Author's collection*

The steam-powered sternwheeler, *Nasookin*, which plied the Kootenay Lakes, BC, was launched in 1913. Oliver Aldridge of Cardston learned his trade as a steam engineer on her. When Ralph Vroom went to the Arrow Lakes area of BC to chase wild horses in the early 1920s, he travelled part way aboard this steamship. *Author's collection*

Another trestle over Mill Creek on the railway line from Pincher Station to Beaver Mines was about two miles northeast of the Mountain Mill trestle. The Lang's Coulee trestle was about as high as the Mountain Mill trestle (Map 7), but only half as long, said old timer Bert Link. According to Glenbow Archives it was 204 feet high and about 1500 feet long. *Glenbow Archives NA-2001-1*

Dominic Cyr, fall 1941, drives his new tractor on his farm two and one-half miles southeast of Pincher Creek He is pulling a combine, a new invention in those days, while harvesting one of his fine fields of grain. A big straw stack in the right middle of this picture indicates that a lot of Dominic's wheat is already threshed and probably delivered to one of the grain elevators beside the CPR tracks at Pincher Station. Frank Slide is visible in the distance (right). *Author's collection*

Three Beaver Mines men in the 1930s are getting ice from a shallow slough near their home. They are using a makeshift inclined plane to load the heavy blocks onto a low sleigh that is pulled by a team of horses. A second team is hitched to an empty sleigh waiting to have it loaded with ice. Having no electricity for a refrigerator people used ice boxes to keep their perishable foods cool in summertime. They stored the ice in sawdust in ice houses. A new block was put into the icebox as needed. *Courtesy S Anderson*

Ruby Vroom hauling ice on stone boat, winter 1916-17. Harold was serving Overseas with the Canadian Expeditionary Forces. Like other women, Ruby dug in and learned how to do a man's work until Harold came home. Wounded in France, Harold returned home before the end of WWI. *Courtesy R Jaggernath*

In 1935 Sonia Chiesa stands in front of the new barn her father built on his homestead on Screwdriver Creek. New barns sprouting up around the countryside were evidence of the prosperity being enjoyed by homesteaders who stuck with the land. Some people carried fond memories of homestead life and referred to the original log cabin where the family lived in cramped quarters as, "The dear old log cabin." *Courtesy Sonia Chiesa Barclay Anderson*

As soon as they were able, settler's built new buildings. First, they built a new barn to keep livestock warm during long, cold spells of winter. Then, they improved their home. This house was built in 1917 by August "Gus" and Mary Schulte Hochstein. With double walls and high ceilings, it may have been an Eatons' Catalogue house. The house replaced the homestead cabin of Robert Kerr on NW 35-4-29-4th. Lester & Doris Therriault Hochstein live here in 2011. *Courtesy E Hochstein*

A note on this photo says 'Lebel House 1913-1914'. It was the home of the Tim Lebel family in Pincher Creek for many years. Mr. Lebel willed the building to the Roman Catholic Order Les Filles de Jesus, who established St. Vincent's Hospital. Bessie, Bill and Marion Vroom were born here. Later, it was sold to the town. After renovations, including the addition of a four-bed maternity ward, it became a modern, municipal hospital. Geordie and Bessie Annand's four children, Edi-May, Evelyn, Dave and James were born in the 'modernized' hospital. In 2011, it's occupied by the Pincher Creek Allied Arts Council. *Courtesy Bertie Jenkins Patriquin*

IT'S OFF TO SCHOOL WE GO!

Early in the homestead era, schools to educate settlers' children were built throughout the Prairie Provinces. Built in a similar design, these schools were generally rectangular in shape. Inside was one large room where as many as 40 wooden desks accommodated children ranging from five and one-half years to 16 or 17 years of age. There was a boys' cloak room and a girls' cloak room and a bucket of water and hand basin for drinking and hand-washing. A heater in one corner provided heat in cold weather. Holes in a seat built over a pit served as an outdoor toilet.

Some pupils had to go as far as five or more miles to reach school. The pupils and teacher walked, rode on horseback or drove a cart pulled by a horse to school in winter and summer, through rain, snow or sleet. Outdoor games like softball, pom-pom pull away and prisoner's base were favourite recess games in spring, summer and fall. Fox and geese and hare-and-hounds were popular winter games. Community and family recreation activities provided weekend fun for the students and their families.

Seen here in 1927, Beauvais School was southwest of Pincher Creek on the south side of Mill Creek. It was first called St. Agnes School. When the school was rebuilt the name was changed to Beauvais School.

(Left to right) Back row: Cicille Cote, Ethel Bishop, Fern Leedham, Elsie Bishop, Eli Therriault. Middle row: Morris Gervais, Edward Lunn, Fred Sandy, Henry Therriault, Wilbrod Gervais. Bottom row: Harold Lunn, Myrtle Sandy, Leonard Cote, Aileen Lunn, Julia Sandy, Hector Therriault. Teacher: Hugh Ross. *Courtesy Hector Cote*

When the Beaver Mines School was in my Uncle Harold and Aunt Ruby Vroom's (Map 3) chicken coop, it was nicknamed "the Chicken Coop School". 1939-1940 students (left to right) Back row: Robert Foster, Mrs. Eda Foster, Joan Kovatch, Wallace "Waddy" Foster holding his mare "Goldie "; Front row: Alan Foster, Vada Hill, May LaGrandeur, Gladys Foster, Mary LaGrandeur. This was taken on Gladys' 9th birthday, May 7, 1940, at Elk Lodge where Waddy was the warden. Joan's father was the warden at Castle River. The LaGrandeur children had to ride about five miles one way to attend this school when they were living at the cow camp in the Castle River Forest Reserve. *Robin LaGrandeur*

(Left to right) Lorna Jacobs, Elaine Jacobs, Betty Annand, Lucille Jacobs, Mervyn Jacobs, Guy Jacobs (small in front) stand in front of Jim Jacob's house, Caldwell, north of Mountain View, in 1915. The five oldest were pupils at Caldwell School. The log cabin of George and Betsy Annand, Sr., was behind this building, to the west. Bringing Betty, they emigrated from Scotland in 1912. They had experience with cattle and draft horses. In 1919 they proved up a homestead in the Drywood district. *Courtesy Elaine Jacobs Nelson*

By the 1940s, rural schools tended to have small enrolments, but there was still a wide variation in size and age of the pupils. 1940 Chipman School students (left to right) Steve Decker (owner of bicycle), Colin Oddie, George Harder (Dave's twin), Hilda Dase, Wanda Davidoff (tall), Helen (surname unknown, with hand over face), Jackie Varley, and teacher Eleanor D'Amico (far right) explains a point. Playing softball against other schools was a favourite sport. *Courtesy Dave Harder*

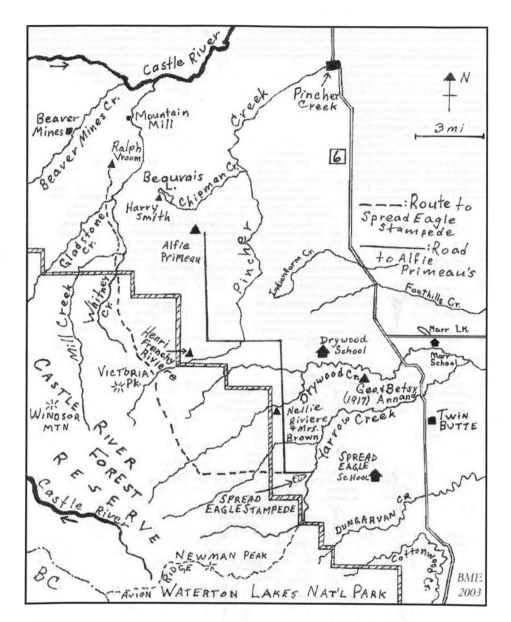

MAP 4 SCHOOLS ALONG the FOOTHILLS of S.W. ALBERTA, 1934
This map is from *The Vrooms of the Foothills, Vol 1: Adventures of My Childhood*, in which I tell of riding to the Spread Eagle Stampede in the summer of 1934. Shown are locations of schools at Beaver Mines (Coalfields School), Pincher Creek, and Twin Butte as well as in the districts of Drywood, Marr and Spread Eagle. Ranches and homesteads shown: George and Betsy Annand, Henri "Frenchy" Riviere, Nellie Gladstone Riviere, Alphie and Alice Riviere Primeau, Ralph and Mollie Tyson Vroom. *Map hand drawn by the Author*

Marjorie Clements (Link) stands in front of the home of her parents, Harry and Margaret Clements, in Pincher Creek in 1933. Marjorie was my first teacher and one of my favourite teachers. She was teaching at Coalfields School when I started on my sixth birthday on January 8, 1933. She and Dave Link eloped the summer of 1934 so Marjorie did not teach me a second year. Dave Link was tall, handsome and easy-going. Marjorie was petite, auburn-haired and vivacious. They were a perfect couple. They lived in a quaint cottage at Mountain Mill, where my brother Don and I as children once rode eight miles each way in late winter to visit my beloved Miss Clements. *Courtesy Ginger Link Reimer*

My grade two teacher (1933-34) Miss Ida Genovese put on very elaborate Christmas concerts. For the December 1933 concert she produced an operetta, "The Sleeping Beauty," which had a large enough cast that almost all of her 40 some pupils had a part to play. I was dressed as one of the fairies that danced around the sleeping princess.

Mom made my dress of white crepe paper and my wings of white gauze trimmed with silver tinsel. In this late spring 1934 picture, I am wearing my costume and holding my pony, Dickie, by the bridle reins. My hair was in long ringlets, which Mom curled by wrapping my hair around long strips of white rags. This was done when my hair was freshly washed and left to dry overnight. *Author's collection*

Pupils of Cyr School, 1927. (Left to right) Back row: Ida Hahn, Margaret "Margie" McWhirter, Ernest Hahn, John Collins; Front row: Norman Hahn, David Hudson, Grace Collins, Essie McWhirter (Cox) 10 years old here, Dorothy Hahn (Cyr), Alice Schultz, Gordon Schoening, Dan Hahn. Cyr School was at the highest elevation of any school in the Pincher Creek School Division. It was 5000 feet above sea level. *Courtesy Essie Cox*

1918 Pleasant (Gladstone) Valley School. (Left to right) Back row: Frank Lippa, Mrs. Crow - teacher, Ella Baker, Minnie Barclay, Bessie Truitt, Gunnar Lund, Karl Nelson, George Liebergall, Charles "Doc" Truitt, John Truitt; Middle row: Cy Truitt, Anne Barclay, Alice Truitt, Sadie Truitt, Jennie Cameron, Cathy Cameron, Alex Barclay, Reggie Baker; Front row: Martha Lippa, Bill Barclay, Jim Cisar, Charles "Buster" Truitt (Missing) Lenora Truitt, Iona Truitt (Map3). *Courtesy Adam "Dutch" & Hazel Truitt*

The original Gladstone Valley School, shown here in 1989, is said to have opened about 1912-1913. However, George Hagglund remembers seeing the date "1906" on the northeast corner of the concrete foundation of this school when he demolished it. Prior to this, Gladstone Valley pupils went to a school located on Charlie Mitchell's homestead, which later was our home ranch. That schoolhouse (Map 3) was built by settler Archie Vroom in 1903-1904 so that his niece and nephews, the children of Oscar and Alena Vroom, would have a school to attend. In 1904, the children, including my dad, came from Nova Scotia with Alena to join their father on his homestead in Beaver Mines Creek Valley (Map 3). *Courtesy F & L Goble*

Dad, my two brothers and I are ready to go riding on a summer's day in 1937. (Left to right) Ralph Vroom on "Fly, Bessie on "Rex", Don on "Laddie" and Bill on "Pickles". During much of the school year we often rode these same ponies to Gladstone Valley School (Map 3). Periodically during the school year, we rode other horses and ponies that Dad wanted to be especially well trained so that he could sell them as gentle saddle horses or children's ponies. *Author's Collection*

One-year-old Anne Russell sits atop "Baby" in front of her home at Skyline Saddle Horses in Waterton Park in 1953. The house was built by George and Betsy Annand in 1924 when they established the "Waterton Lakes Dairy". Anne's parents, Andy and Kay (Riggall) rented saddle horses for day trips to the mountain lakes in the Park. In the fall they took hunting parties on extended pack trips in the mountains. Anne attended Park View School as did her mother before her. *Courtesy Anne Russell Raabe & John Russell*

Park View School pupils and siblings, teacher and parents, 1924. (Left to right) back row: unknown woman, Magrethe "Gada" Anderson, Marius Anderson, Teacher Miss Margaret McGuire , Nancy Williams, Kenneth Williams and Phyllis Williams.

Front row: Helga Anderson, Katenka Anderson, Anna Anderson, Helen Pedersen, Madge Pedersen, Alma Pedersen, Harry Pedersen, Mrs. Johanne Orslar Pedersen holding baby Esther Pedersen (married Douglas Hewitt of North Fork district). The Pedersen youngsters in the picture are children of Klem and Johanne Pedersen. *Courtesy H & G Bruns*

In 1930, my cousins, children of Dominic and Marion Vroom Cyr, rode to school in a two-wheeled cart pulled by a single horse. (Left to right) Rita (6 yrs), Vera (8 yrs), Esther (11 yrs), Eugene (13 yrs), and Adeline (15 yrs) attended St. Michael's School. In fair weather they walked to school taking a shortcut across a neighbour's field. Marie Alberta had finished school already. *Courtesy Adeline Cyr Robbins*

Pincher Creek High School (PCHS) students (left to right) Betty Holmes and Isabelle Main, stand with Mrs. Sarah (George) Ballantyne in front of Ballantyne's Store in Beaver Mines on May 24, 1934. They're ready to return to school for another week. The two girls and Jo Ballantyne were boarding with Mrs. Gray in Pincher Creek. Sarah holds a box lunch for the girls to eat en route.

Alma "Jo" who took the picture also attended PCHS. She graduated from the University of Alberta in Edmonton, becoming a high-school teacher. *Courtesy Jo Ballantyne Johnson*

The PCHS dormitory enabled students from rural schools in the Pincher Creek School Division to attend high school in town. About 40 students, 20 boys and 20 girls, ate, slept and studied at the dormitory during the week. They went home for weekends.

In the spring of 1942, roommates are (left to right) Helen Burns, Inga Bechtal, Bessie Vroom, Dorothy Holroyd, and Wanda Dase. We're relaxing on the grass west of the dormitory, fondly called the "Dorm". *Author's Collection*

The end of the school year meant a class hike to a favourite picnic spot. In June 1943, the grade four class of Pincher Creek Public School poses on a rock ledge along Pincher Creek, an area fondly called "up the canyon". At that time, the Canyon was about two miles west of the school. My brother, Bill Vroom stands on the right of the group. *Author's Collection*

Robert Kerr School 1925. (Left to right) Back row: Marjorie Shaw, Kathleen "Kay" Carpenter, Willie (Bill) Carpenter, Velda Smith, Kathleen Newman (partially obscured), Dorothy Shaw, Margaret Dennis, Annie McRae, Edith "Toots" Jack; Middle row: Myrtle Hardy, Olive Hardy (partially obscured), Pearl Jack (eyes closed), Jack Dennis, John Bakie; Front row (l to r) Esther Hardy, Frances Dennis, Marion Bird, Irene Jack (head down), Carl Hardy, Willie Hardy

The school faced east. The barn was in the NW corner of school yard. The girls' and boys' outhouses were on the north side to the east of the barn, they were separated by a coal shed which held fuel for the "puffing Billy" heater. *Courtesy Edith "Toots" Jack Hochstein*

Four schoolteacher friends stand arm and arm in Ontario in 1902. (Left to right) Miss Anderson, Marietta "Etta" Irwin, Percy Owens and Sybil Jewell. In 1906, Etta Irwin came west, first to Saskatchewan and then to Pincher Creek.

In 1907-08, Etta taught at Crook School. In 1908, she married rancher Malcolm McRae of the Drywood district. Etta was a skilled photographer. She built a dark room and developed and printed her own photos. *Courtesy Kay McRae Leigh*

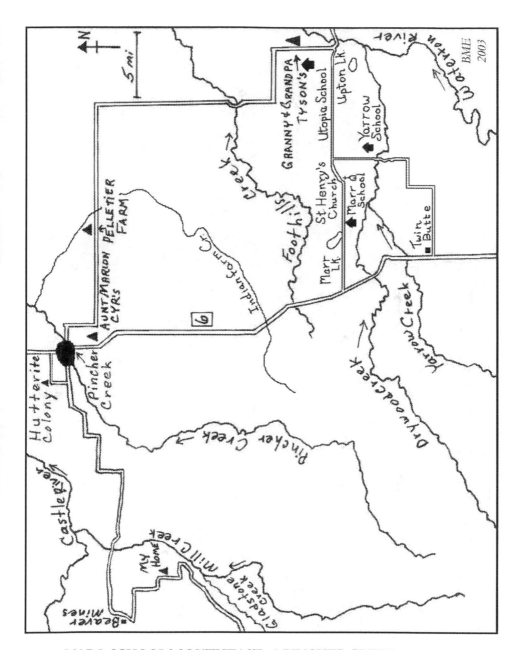

MAP 5 SCHOOLS SOUTHEAST of PINCHER CREEK, circa 1933

This map is from *The Vrooms of the Foothills: Adventures of My Childhood.* Shown are: Marr School, Yarrow School, Utopia School and St. Henry's Roman Catholic Church. Also, the farm of Aunt Marion (Vroom) and Uncle Dominic Cyr, and Granny and Grandpa George and Mary Tyson. *Map hand drawn by the Author*

Of the schools in the Pincher Creek School Division, the Twin Butte School had one of the larger enrolments. Pupils in Twin Butte School in spring 1923 were (Left to right) Back row: Ed Schempp, Clyde Hole born 1907, Myron Cox born 1907 (brother of Orville), Gladys McRae (Mrs. James Taylor) teacher, Helen Faull, Mabel Schempp, Berdella "Birdie" Cox born 1910 (Orville's sister), Orville Cox, Ronald Hole born 1911.

Middle row: (6 children of varying sizes) Ila Terrill, Ethel Hole born 1909, Hilaria Bonertz (became mother of Mark Leins), Inez McCarthy, Walter Bogart (small boy), unknown small boy. Front row: Winnie Hole born 1913, Jim Upton, Fred Hole born 1915, Melvin Cox, Helen Schempp, Rita Bogart (striped dress), Wilfred Schempp, unknown boy, Emery Bonertz.

This photo was taken in front of the Bill McWhirter homestead house. The mother of the Cox children was Mary Aldridge, whose father Bill Aldridge first commercialized the sale of oil from what became Oil City, Waterton Park. *Courtesy Essie McWhirter Cox*

Physical education was one of the favourite times of day for rural school children. Circa 1937-1938, pupils at Utopia School carry gymnastics into the recess period by forming a human pyramid.

The five biggest and strongest pupils form the bottom row; the four next-sized ones form the second row; the three next-sized pupils form the third row; the two smallest pupils in the class perch on top to complete the pyramid. *Courtesy Bessie Thomas Halton*

Grades 1 – 11, Waterton Park School, March 1931. (Left to right) Back row: Miss Inez McCarthy, teacher; unknown; Bert Pittaway; *George "Geordie" Annand; Jack Carnell; Stan Dilatush; Clint Goble, Jack Pittaway, Frank Goble, Wallace Ellison. Middle Row, left to right: Joy Goble; *Helen Dickson; Ethel Hole; *Isobel Morrow; Audrey McAllister; *Beatrice Morrow; Phyllis Anderson; Dennis Pittaway; Sheldon Strate; unknown; Miss Isabel Morrison, teacher. Front row, left to right: George Frederickson; Orene Strate; Cam Dickson; *Jean Dickson; Dorothy Udell; Gladys Strate; four unknown girls; Bob Matkin; Doug Matkin; Bill Gregory; Roy McKenzie. *Students in the first, 1925-26, school. *Author's Collection*

September 1947, Junior Room pupils, Waterton School, on a log bridge across Bertha Creek while on a school hike to Bertha Lake. Photo by teacher Bessie Vroom. (Left to right) Standing: Shirley Albiston, Susan Going, Bitsey Aitken, Merna Going.

Seated: Ken Allred, David Goble, Jack Gladstone, Michael Carnell, Brian Reeves, Diane Allison, Dorothy Allison, Rae Baker, Tom Aitken, Judy Going, Elaine Black, Valerie Ayris; Dick Allison (hidden), Helen Leavitt, Eldon Wacher. *Author's Collection*

Beaver Creek was often unsafe for skating because of its continual flow and the frequent chinooks. Despite this, about 1930, a group of young people skate energetically along the creek on a track they cleared of snow. *Courtesy Katherine Bruce*

The young people who lived in Cowley were a little better off with regards to ice-skating than those who lived around Beaver Mines. The Cowley young people had a good-sized pond nearby where the ice would freeze to a depth that was safe for skating. Here in the 1940s one of the children of C. J. and Mrs. Freda Graham Bundy gets a lift up after a spill. Skating costumes fashionable in the 1940s are seen in this picture. *Courtesy Jean McEwen Burns*

Windemere Lake on the W. D. McDowall farm was a perfect spot for wiener roasts and skating parties. The lake froze solidly early in the winter. Here in the early 1930s, a group including Ronald, Anthony and Michael Bruce practice their puck passing skills. *Courtesy K Bruce*

My sister, Marion, feeding a cub, circa spring 1947. Unknown to Bill (left), a mother bear he shot had two cubs, which he found when he dug out the den. He took the cubs home. Mom rigged up a baby bottle to feed them cow's milk. When they became too big, the cubs were given to the Calgary Zoo. *Author's Collection*

This family post card shows a close-up view of the top tower of Castle Mountain, renamed Windsor Mountain. Windsor Mountain looks very challenging from the east. However, the west side of the mountain is a safe, though somewhat strenuous, climb. Climbing parties often reach the base of the tower, but few have climbed to the top of the tower.

In my book, *The Vrooms of the Foothills: Adventures of My Childhood*, is a description of my experience climbing to the base of this tower in 1938, when I was 11 years old (Map 2). Guided by my Dad, I climbed it along with my cousin Vera Cyr Gingras of Pincher Creek, and my brothers, Don and Bill. *Author's Collection*

Gerry Hutchinson, student minister at Fishburn United Church during the summers of 1940 and 1941, took a great interest in the youth of the district. In June 1941 he took a group of boys to see Bert Riggall, a well known naturalist and mountain guide who operated a pack horse outfit in SW Alberta.

(Left to right) Back row: Alfred Simpson (tall), Bert Riggall, unknown in white hat; Front row: Freeman Fitzpatrick, Bob Thomas, Gerry Hutchinson, Bruce Slater, Sammy McAuley, Billy Vroom, Jimmy Taylor. Listening to Bert describe the flora and fauna along the trail to Blakiston Falls in Waterton Park influenced Bob Thomas to work as an outfitter as his life's work. *Courtesy Bob Thomas*

In 1959 my daughters, Evelyn Annand (left) and Edi-May, hold the little skunks they caught. The babies were in a flower bed trailing their mother beside our home in Waterton Park. While I focused my camera, Evelyn rushed forward and picked up one. Edi-May had no trouble catching the other bewildered animal, much to the delight of both girls. *Author's Collection*

My son Jim Annand, summer of 1966. He's holding a gopher (Columbia ground squirrel) in fishing net. Jim helped his sister Evelyn capture the gopher by luring it into a pipe baited with left over pancakes from Sunday breakfast.

Jim held the fishing net over one end of the pipe. Evelyn hoisted up the other end causing the terrified gopher to slide down the pipe and out the other end. Jim jumped up, triumphantly holding the imprisoned gopher. The gopher was released unharmed, and went on to participate in the "catching" game on other Sunday mornings. Pancakes were its reward. *Author's Collection*

East View School near Drumheller, AB, was the first school where I taught after graduating from Calgary Normal School in December 1944 at 17 years of age. To become a school teacher, I attended Normal School in Calgary from September 1 to December 15, 1944. In that time, I earned my Wartime Emergency Teaching Certificate. That was a special certificate necessitated by the teacher shortage caused when so many male teachers joined the Armed Forces in WWII. To qualify for a Permanent Teaching Certificate I had to teach for at least two full years and take additional courses at Summer School at the University of Alberta in Edmonton in 1945 and 1946.

I started teaching at East View School in the Drumheller School Division on January 3, 1945. Here some of my East View School pupils demonstrate their skill at skijoring. Left to right: Shirley Edwards on horseback holding Miss Vroom's saddle horse, "Black Sambo," and Jim Andrew on skis waiting his turn at skijoring. Shirley MacNaughton rides her saddle horse along the road while pulling her sister, Janet, and another of my pupils, Allan MacKinnon, who are skijoring in the ditch.

The next year I taught at Livingstone School, also near Drumheller. In 1947-1948, I taught at Waterton Park School in the Cardston School Division. I qualified for my Permanent Teaching Certificate June 30, 1948. *Author's Collection*

FIRESIDE HOBBIES

W hile living in relative isolation, people engaged in a number of hobbies. Women and girls pursued photography, painting in oils and water colours, rag rug-making, knitting, crocheting, and designing and sewing their own and their children's clothes. Boys made model airplanes and model farms. Men decorated their leather clothing and made hand-tooled designs on saddles and bridles for their horses. Children made up new games to play and variations of old games. Pictures in this chapter emphasize the creativity and artistic ability of the people of southwestern Alberta.

Etta B. Platt (centre) of Waterton Park and two girls from New York City in Glacier National Park, 1937. Etta is wearing a leather touring suit she made for herself. By 1940, Mrs. Platt had painted this car a silver colour. The locals called it "the Silver Streak." Etta was very self-sufficient. She could change a flat tire and did all the tune-ups on her car. *Author's Collection*

Making clothing decorated with fancy embroidering and trimmed with handmade lace for their young children was a favourite fireside hobby of many women in the early 1900s.

This charming 1910 picture shows three of the children of Mr. and Mrs. Fred Link, ranchers at Mountain Mill west of Pincher Creek for many years (Map 7). The children are: Charlie (standing at rear), Dave (seated left), Bert (seated right). Photo taken at Beaver Mines. *Courtesy Bill Link*

In addition to making clothes from leather, Mrs. Etta B. Platt also decorated clothing with embroidered pictures. She designed and sewed the clothes herself. First, she drew the pictures free hand, usually in a western motif. Then, she embroidered them using wool of a variety of bright colours in an intricate cross-stitch design. An unknown cowboy models a complete riding suit (vest and batwing chaps) made by Mrs. Platt. A note on the back of the picture says, "The vest was raffled off at (the) 'War Hut' last summer. 1941." Raffles at the Waterton War Hut raised funds for local soldiers overseas in WWII. *Author's Collection*

The vest below illustrates how Mrs. Platt designed and constructed colourful cross-stitched clothing. She drew a picture on a square of burlap about 8 inches by 8 inches, then hand-sewed each square onto cotton fabric forming the front, back and sleeves of the garment. When she sewed the various parts together it became a sturdy garment. *Author's Collection*

This 1930s scatter rug, hand-embroidered by Etta Platt of Waterton Park, using colourful wool, features a centre picture of Upper Waterton Lake, as viewed from the Prince of Wales Hotel. Around it are various birds and animals found in the Park. *Author's Collection*

1915, the sons of Edward and Mabel Noyes Bruce living on the Roodee Ranch (Map 7), on the Castle River northeast of Mountain Mill. (Left to right) Michael, Anthony, Ronald. Their outfits were lovingly made by their mother. *Courtesy H Grace*

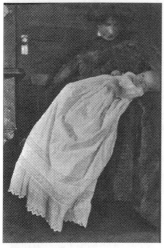

One can only guess at the hours of patient work it took to crochet the deep layers of lace that adorn this child's christening gown. Mabel Bruce holds Michael, her second child, on her lap when they were living near Cluny, AB, in 1911. Michael lies on a fur throw given to Mabel by the chief of the nearby Siksika tribe. *Courtesy K Bruce*

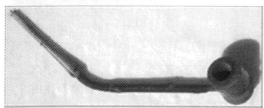

Sometimes my dad visited with his friends on the Peigan Reserve at Brocket, AB, where Dad also wintered our herd of horses at times. Occasionally families from the Peigan Reserve visited us on our ranch at Beaver Mines.

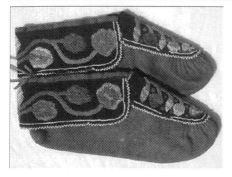

Whenever they were in need of food, they could always count on Mom and Dad to feed them. This long-stemmed wooden pipe and beautifully beaded adult-sized moccasins were gifts from friends on the Reserve. *Author's Collection.*

In this undated photo, Mrs. Joe Primeau works at her spinning wheel at their home east of the Alberta Ranch on a sunny afternoon. All fireside crafts require a lot of time, patience and skill. One of the more demanding activities was spinning raw sheep's wool into yarn. The yarn was then used for knitting various warm winter garments for family members. *Used with the kind permission of The Archives of The Pincher Creek and District Historical Society.*

Mrs. Harper stands on the porch of her boarding house in Pincher Creek, 1913. She boarded rural students attending high school. Etta Irwin McRae and her small daughter, Kay, stand at the gate. Malcolm waits for his wife. Etta developed and printed her photos.

Years later Constance Holroyd used the same process. Her son, Jack, described, "You mixed up fixer in one pan and developer in another and a third pan held water for washing prints. A piece of light-sensitive paper was fixed in a frame, much like a picture frame, against glass. The negative was put in first, then the paper. You put in a back, which sandwiched the negative and paper in place. This all had to be done in the dark so as not to expose the sensitive paper before you were ready." *Courtesy Kay McRae Leigh*

Mabel Bruce was an early resident of the Pincher Creek area who was a skilled artist. Mabel painted this delicate watercolour of the Mountain Mill Church in 1914 (Map 7). She gave this miniature to her friend Sarah McJanet (George) Ballantyne as a Christmas card. The Bruces had just moved to the Roodee Ranch east of Mountain Mill. The church was built through a community effort in 1906. *Courtesy D & L McClelland*

Eaton's Beauty dolls were cherished possessions of little girls in the 1930s. Elva's mother, Sarah McJanet Ballantyne, a tailoress by profession, made this doll's clothes. Elva called her doll "Suzy." One Christmas my parents, thinking that I should have some "little girl" toys to play with, bought me an Eaton's Beauty doll. My brother Don designed a pattern, cut out and sewed a suit for my new doll. The suit had a navy blue skirt and bright red jacket with tiny brass buttons. *Courtesy Elva McClelland*

Building models out of balsa wood was a favourite pastime in the 1930s. Kits were available. Michael Bruce made this model farm. *Courtesy K. Bruce*

In 1933, I am riding my child-sized saddle and guiding my goat "Smokey" with a halter that Dad made for him. Dad was skilled at leather work and harness making. He kept our riding gear oiled and in good repair. Robin LaGrandeur recalls playing hooky from Coalfields School by going "over to Vrooms and playing with the goats." *Courtesy Don Vroom*

In the 1940s and 1950s, snowshoes were still important gear for wardens in Waterton Park. Here are four types of homemade snowshoes demonstrated by warden Bert Pittaway while conducting a school for new wardens. Wardens chose the appropriate snowshoes for the snow conditions, how heavy a load they were carrying and/or how fast they wanted to travel. *Courtesy Anne Pittaway McKenzie*

The three children of C.J. and Freda Graham Bundy in Hallowe'en or masquerade costume in about the 1930s. (Left to right) Jack, about 4 years; Barbara, about 6 years; Clare, about 3 years. The costumes were lovingly made by their mother, Freda Graham Bundy (1895-1962). Freda was a journalist and author of note. Most of her large body of literary work, including short stories, novels, biographies, and feature articles are held in the Glenbow Museum Archives. When I knew her in the 1950s, Freda was the district correspondent for The Lethbridge Herald. *Courtesy Jean McEwen Burns*

About 1943, Mrs. Etta Platt (left) of Waterton Park and Bessie Vroom are ready for the Pincher Creek parade. Mrs. Platt's horse is adorned with a beaded martingale handmade by Peigan Indians of Brocket, AB. We are wearing chaps and vests featuring original pictures drawn and embroidered in wool cross stitching by Mrs. Platt. *Author's Collection*

Detail of the beadwork on the martingale on Mrs. Platt's horse (above). This martingale was owned by Ralph and Mollie Vroom. Dad traded goods of equal value, maybe even a horse, for the martingale. *Author's Collection*

In 1944 my mother made this lovely new spring coat of a very soft light blue wool material. Teenage girls wore gloves; bobby socks were also in style. Until I finished school, my mother sewed most of my clothes. When making something different, she used a pattern and followed the instructions carefully. When I married I sewed clothing for myself and for my children. *Author's Collection*

(Left) This was my first evening gown, a turquoise net princess style dress over a pale green taffeta slip. My mother created it using the Singer machine that had belonged to her mother, Mary Tyson. The slip was made by remodeling another long dress. I wore this gown to the Pincher Creek New Year's Eve Fireman's Ball on December 31, 1943. My (future) bridesmaid, Robina Hewitt (Peterson), wore her first evening gown to the same Ball. I took my gown to "Aunt Alena" Hewitt's, where Robina stayed during her high school years, and we practiced walking in our gowns. Our dates for the evening also practiced walking and dancing with us. *Author's Collection*

Geordie Annand and I were married in All Saints Anglican Church in Waterton on September 11, 1948. Adeline Cyr (Gerald) Robbins of Pincher Creek decorated this beautiful three-tiered wedding cake. Nellie Hunter Goble Hadfield helped me bake the cake.

Our wedding reception was held at the home of Gerald and Nellie Hadfield in Waterton Park. Geordie is on the right and I'm in the background, just before cutting the first slice. Later that evening, the wedding party danced to the music of Mart Kenney and his Western Gentlemen at the Waterton Dance Pavilion.

My daughter, Edi-May, used the cake topper on her wedding cake when she married Wayne Smithies in 1971, also in All Saints Anglican Church in Waterton. Edi-May still has the topper and my wedding dress among her cherished possessions. Photo by Frank Goble. *Courtesy Frank & Linnea Hagglund Goble*

Leon Levesque chose bronze as a medium to express his artistic talents. He was particularly adept at portraying historical scenes such as this. The bronze created by Leon from this scene shows a night rider helping to keep a herd of Texas longhorn cattle moving steadily north along the trail to the railway. The most likely setting for this scene is somewhere along the storied Chisholm trail which led from Texas north to the railway that ran east to Chicago. *Courtesy Leon Levesque*

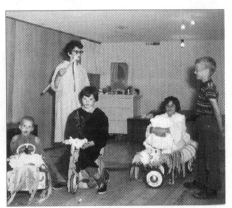

The children of Geordie and Bessie Annand, and guest Patti Gannon, are play-acting in the basement of our home in Waterton Park in the summer of 1963. Left to right are: Jim Annand; Edi-May Annand, directing; Evelyn Annand; Patti Gannon; David Annand. The children wrote the play themselves then produced it for their own amusement.

Don and Anne Gannon of Regina and their family spent their holidays in Waterton Park for about 10 summers. They stayed in Annands' Vimyvue Cabins across from Lake Linnet. *Author's Collection*

Girl Guides, Brownies, Cubs and Boy Scouts learn basic personal, home and survival skills. Through the badge system, children in these organizations get a taste of various hobbies, which years later may develop into a passion.

Geordie's and my children are in front of our home across from Lake Linnet in Waterton Park, during the summer of 1962. Brownie Evelyn Annand (centre) and Girl Guide Edi-May Annand stand with their brothers, David (left side) and James on his new tricycle. Evelyn and Edi-May were new to Brownies and Girl Guides. A few years later Evelyn "flew up" to Girl Guides; Edi-May received her All Round (Blue) Cord; and David joined Cub Scouts. *Author's Collection*

Geordie's and my children going for an early morning "ride" in a cardboard box train in our living room, about 1962. Left to right: David, engineer; Evelyn, fireman; Jim, passenger; Edi-May, conductor. We got a large order of groceries from Hofer & Wood Food Store in Lethbridge once a month. There were lots of boxes for imaginary vehicles of various descriptions. *Author's Collection*

By 1964 Edi-May Annand had reached her goal. She was qualified to attend a Girl Guide Heritage Camp. These camps were held three years before Canada's Centennial Year, as a run-up to Centennial celebrations.

All Girl Guides in Canada competed for selection. Twenty-four were chosen in each province. Two attended the heritage camp in their home province. The rest went two-by-two to other territories and provinces. Edi-May went to the Heritage Camp on Lake Manitoba, MN. Here, just prior to leaving for camp, Edi-May holds her younger brother, Jim, on her lap. Her badges including a camper's badge and a little housekeeping badge are neatly stitched onto her uniform. *Author's Collection*

Young people love to have a space of their own where they can act out their fantasies. Jim Annand, left, and Keith Rogers, right, pretend to be disc jockeys in the attic of Keith's home in Waterton Park in about 1969. They spent countless hours hunched over their makeshift furniture enjoying the popular music of the day in the privacy of their den.

Keith's father, Harold, was the senior room teacher in Waterton Park School, senior room, from 1962 to 1971. *Author's Collection*

During the two years that my mother, Mollie Vroom, resided in the Perley Rehabilitation Centre in Ottawa she pursued her girlhood passion for drawing and painting. Mollie chose the medium of oil painting and did a number of paint-by-number pictures. As Mollie painted, she blended the colours slightly over the lines so that there was not a ridge in between colours. When finished the paintings looked like they had been done freehand. *Courtesy Evelyn Annand Lailey*

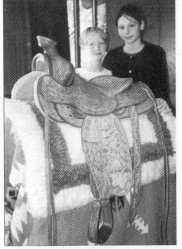

Bill Vroom, a long-time warden in Banff National Park, designed, stamped and made this intricately hand-tooled All-round Roper saddle in his spare time in his home in Banff. Bill, a rancher and horseman at heart, learned his saddle-making skills while working for Riley and McCormick Western Wear in Calgary before he joined the Park Warden Service. Vanessa Annand (left) and Megan Lailey (right), two of Bill's great-nieces, stand beside the saddle in 1998. *Courtesy Dan Vroom & Doreen Lund*

Elva Ballantyne McClelland, in 1988, studies the pattern and layout of an assembled quilt that is ready for quilting. The quilt on its frame is in the Mountain Mill United Church, in the Mill Creek valley east of Beaver Mines (Map 7). Elva sewed leftover corduroy pieces into a sturdy picnic blanket for her son and daughter-in-law, Doug and Lee Gingras McClelland. Others of the Mountain Mill United Church Women helped Elva put the heavy quilt in her frames. The backing is an old style flannel sheet. That, along with the quilt batting and the corduroy top, made it too heavy to do regular quilting, so the women tied it. *Courtesy Elva Ballantyne McClelland*

INDEPENDENT SOULS

One quarter section of land was not big enough to provide a living for a family. Some homesteaders did not want to be farmers or ranchers on a long term basis. Other families really wanted to make their homestead their home, so they bought land from nearby homesteaders. The people who sold their homesteads often went into business in a nearby town.

Also, as homesteaders' family members grew in number the older children had to seek a living elsewhere. They, too, often went into business supplementing their income as best they could. Chapter 7 talks about the many and varied businesses founded by these "independent souls".

Built in 1921 near Lake Linnet, Waterton Park, by John "Jack" Bevan, Outfitter, 'Lochvue' (left) was sold in 1924 to John and Malvina Morris. Their sons Scottie, Cliff, Eugene, Billy and Clarence operated Morris Bros. Guides & Outfitters. In 1944, Martin and "Slim" Wacher bought the Morris Bros. operation. Shortly after, the Parks administration decided they didn't want horses stabled on this property. In June 1944, George and Betsy Annand traded properties with Martin & Leona Wacher. The Wacher Lakeside Dude Ranch later became the site of the Russell Skyline Saddle Horses in the 1950s (Map 6).

George and Betsy converted Lochvue to be their residence and included four individual rental rooms with a shared bathroom. In 1945, they built Vimyvue Cabins (right) with two fully-equipped housekeeping cabins, on the site of the old Morris bunkhouse. These made a viable tourist rental business which Betsy operated. This income supplemented George's salary as government storekeeper for the Department of Mines and Resources at 'Headquarters' behind Lochvue and Vimyvue. *Author's Collection*

After teaching just a few years, I was another school teacher snapped up by a local man. My fiancé, Geordie Annand, and I strike a loving pose on Main Street in Waterton Park townsite.

I taught at Waterton Park School in 1947-48. Then I worked at the Waterton Lakes Hotel and Chalets for the summer of 1948 to save enough money to pay for my wedding reception in September. Linda Hadfield, 2 year old daughter of Gerry and Nellie Hunter Goble Hadfield, stands looking up at us.

For twenty summers afterwards, I helped my mother-in-law, Betsy, rent Lochvue and Vimyvue to tourists. *Author's Collection*

Betsy Penny Annand came to Canada from Scotland in the spring of 1912 along with her husband, George Annand and daughter, Betty. A son, Geordie, was born in Cardston, AB, in 1915. Initially, George and Betsy worked for the Jacobs Bradshaw ranch at Caldwell, AB. In 1919 they 'proved up' on their homestead on Drywood Creek, west of Twin Butte. They had many business interests – they were market gardeners, ran a dairy in Waterton, and rented tourist accommodations, Lochvue and Vimyvue Cabins, in Waterton for a number of years. In 1938 Betsy took her only trip to the old country. She sailed on the Canadian Pacific S.S. *Duchess of York* to Scotland to visit friends and relatives. This is her passport photo. *Author's Collection*

This idyllic setting was George and Betsy Annand's dairy camp in Waterton Park for the summers of 1920-1924 (Map 6). Located beside Pass Creek (Blakiston Brook), the camp was built on the flat created by the western side of the first bridge over 'lower' Pass Creek. In the background is Mt. Galwey. "Muley" is the Holstein cow in the foreground. The cows were pastured on the Badlands. Early each morning and in the evening, Betty Annand rode her beloved pony Mollie to herd the cows. Betsy also kept chickens at the dairy camp and sold eggs and dressed chickens to customers in Waterton townsite. *Courtesy Betty Annand Baker*

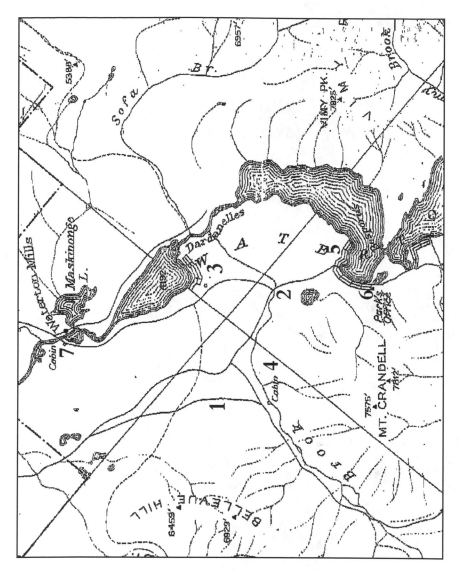

MAP 6   WATERTON LAKES NATIONAL PARK, 1918

1. Oil Trail leading from Pincher Creek to Oil City on Cameron Creek; **2.** George & Betsy Annand Waterton Lakes Dairy camp, summers 1920-1924; **3.** "Cedar" cabin warden station on Knight's Lake built 1915; **4.** Pass Creek warden cabin built 1918; **5.** George and Betsy Annand home 1924-1944; Martin and John 'Slim' Wacher's Lakeside Dude Ranch; Andy and Kay Riggall Russell's Skyline Saddle Horses; **6.** "Pop" Harwood post office 1916-1927; Geordie and Bessie Annand residence 1951-1969; **7.** Waterton River warden cabin built 1916. Notes on map by Edi-May Annand Smithies. 1918 Map by M.P. Bridgland, Geodetic Survey of Canada. *Courtesy Glenbow Archives*

In the fall of 1924, George and Betsy Annand and their children, Betty and Geordie, moved permanently into Waterton Park. They built a log home and dairy barn on the north shore of Middle Waterton Lake where they operated the Waterton Lakes Dairy until 1927 (Map 6). It was the only continuously operated dairy ever located in the Park. By the 1950s, this property became Skyline Saddle Horses owned by Andy and Kay Riggall Russell. This ad is from *The Lethbridge Herald,* August 7, 1925. Their daughter, Betty, delivered milk on her pony, "Mollie." Two 5-gallon cans of milk hung from the saddle horn, one on each side of Mollie. As she rode along the streets, Betty filled containers people brought out to her and charged them for the amount of milk they received. *Author's Collection*

The swift water of Mill Creek turned the water wheel which powered the first grist mill in Alberta built at Mountain Mill in the fall of 1880, shown here. Later, diverted water operated the McLaren sawmill. The location of the grist mill and sawmill are on Map 7. *T.C. Weston / Library and Archives Canada/ PA-050772*

In 1881, the Indian Department decided the Mountain Mill sawmill was a failure in training Indians in modern work. The mill and timber limits were sold to Senator Peter McLaren of Ottawa (Map 7).

These grinding stones were used to make flour from wheat for farmers and ranchers at the Mountain Mill grist mill. In the 1960s, Bert Link removed these stones from Mill Creek and donated them to the Kootenai Brown Pioneer Village in Pincher Creek. *Courtesy Bill Link*

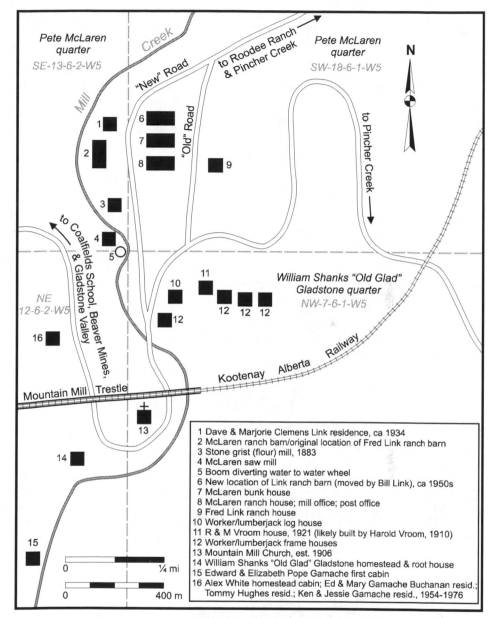

Pete McLaren
quarter
SE-13-6-2-W5

Creek

"New" Road

to Roodee Ranch
& Pincher Creek

Pete McLaren
quarter
SW-18-6-1-W5

N

Mill

"Old" Road

to Pincher Creek →

1

2

6

7

8

9

3

4

5

to Coalfields School, Beaver Mines,
& Gladstone Valley

NE
12-6-2-W5

11

10

12

12 12 12

William Shanks "Old Glad"
Gladstone quarter
NW-7-6-1-W5

16

Kootenay   Alberta   Railway

Mountain Mill Trestle

13

14

15

1 Dave & Marjorie Clemens Link residence, ca 1934
2 McLaren ranch barn/original location of Fred Link ranch barn
3 Stone grist (flour) mill, 1883
4 McLaren saw mill
5 Boom diverting water to water wheel
6 New location of Link ranch barn (moved by Bill Link), ca 1950s
7 McLaren bunk house
8 McLaren ranch house; mill office; post office
9 Fred Link ranch house
10 Worker/lumberjack log house
11 R & M Vroom house, 1921 (likely built by Harold Vroom, 1910)
12 Worker/lumberjack frame houses
13 Mountain Mill Church, est. 1906
14 William Shanks "Old Glad" Gladstone homestead & root house
15 Edward & Elizabeth Pope Gamache first cabin
16 Alex White homestead cabin; Ed & Mary Gamache Buchanan resid.;
   Tommy Hughes resid.; Ken & Jessie Gamache resid., 1954-1976

0   ¼ mi

0   400 m

MAP 7   VILLAGE OF MOUNTAIN MILL, circa 1880-1976
Shown are: ranch barn/original location of Fred Link ranch; stone grist (flour) mill, 1883; McLaren saw mill; boom diverting water to water wheel; McLaren ranch house; R. and M. Vroom house, 1921; Mountain Mill Church, est. 1906; Wm. Shanks "Old Glad" Gladstone's homestead. *Illustration by Edi-May Smithies, Cartography by Shelley McConnell*

Clothed in modest white uniforms, six young women who were maids at the Prince of Wales Hotel, Waterton Park, pose for the photographer. Betty Annand (far left, front row) was among the first people hired to work at the new, luxury hotel when it opened in July 1927.

Betty married George Baker, one of the pioneer businessmen in Waterton Park. They operated Park Transport Company and the Cameron Lake Cabins, Store and Bungalows for a number of years. Their grandson, Brian and Lauren Baker and family still operate a business in Waterton in 2011. *Courtesy Betty Annand Baker*

Many male employees also kept the Prince of Wales Hotel running smoothly. In 1927 the bellhops stand with head bellman, Vic Harrison (second from left). Geordie Annand is third from right. Vic was head bellman from 1927 to 1942. They are on the south side of this grand hotel which has a spectacular panorama of Upper Waterton Lake. *Courtesy Betty Annand Baker*

It takes an energetic crew to run an outfit dedicated to luxury service for adventurers seeking relaxation in Canada's great outdoors.

These cowboys are with Andy & Kay Riggall Russell's Skyline Saddle Horses (Map 6), Waterton Park, in 1956. (Left to right) Charlie Russell (15 years old), Don Lancaster, Richard "Dick" Russell (17 years old), Andy Russell, proprietor, Don Brestler, Ray Woodward and Dave Simpson, foreman. *Courtesy John Russell*

Bert Riggall, an entrepreneur who was one of Alberta's foremost mountain guides, outfitters and photographers, stands with a client on the edge of a deep canyon in the heart of the Rocky Mountains in southwest Alberta. Bert was very knowledgeable about the names of flora and fauna in the Rocky Mountains of S.W. Alberta and S.E. BC. He was always keen to impart his knowledge to other people. Bert's handwriting on the back of this photo states: "Looking West from summit of Clarke Range near Hawk's Nest. Showing head of Castle River, Great Divide and S.E. British Columbia." *Courtesy K Bruce*

F. W. Doubt Livery Stable, Blairmore, AB, 1901. W.F. "Bill" Doubt (on horse), F.W. "Fred" Doubt (in carriage holding reins) and Isabella "Bella" Doubt (far left in rear). In 1903, Fred and Bella homesteaded SW-12-6-2-W5, west of Mountain Mill. Fred was the first chairman of Coalfields school board, just east of Beaver Mines.

Another entrepreneur, Dominic Cyr, who married my beloved Aunt Marion Vroom Cyr, also owned a livery stable as well as a butcher shop in Beaver Mines in 1913. The livery stable burned down in 1915. *Courtesy Jane-Ellen Doubt*

When George and Betsy Annand first operated a dairy in Waterton in 1920, they came only in the summer. Their camp was at the west side of the first bridge over 'lower' Pass Creek (Map 6). Betsy ran a small business - a herd of dairy cattle and flock of chickens. She supplied fresh milk and eggs to residents and visitors in the Park. They also brought in vegetables from their farm on the Belly River. Here at the Pass Creek camp, Betsy keeps a sharp eye on her flock of chickens. George was one of the first men hired in 1926 by Doug Oland to build the Prince of Wales Hotel. George worked as a carpenter. My son, Jim Annand, still has his handsaw. *Courtesy B Baker*

When Angelo and Osanna Chiesa came to Canada, Angelo worked in a coal mine in Michel, BC. Here he stands with their chickens. When they moved to their homestead north of Beaver Mines in 1917, they were market gardeners, selling vegetables, dressed chickens, butter and sausages to customers "up the Pass." *Courtesy S Anderson*

Like the Beaver Mines General Store, the Twin Butte General Store and its post office in early days was the hub of life for families living on remote ranches in the area (Map 4). People gathered in the post office on mail days to exchange family news and pick up a few groceries.

Here in 2010, the Twin Butte General Store is still the community's centre and an attractive rest stop beside the highway from Pincher Creek to Waterton Park. Jenny Davis, the congenial proprietor, offers a cheery gift shop, homemade Mexican food in the bright dining room and a stunning view of the Rocky Mountains. *Courtesy Edi-May Smithies*

After the closing of Oil City post office in 1907, one was operated (1908-1916) by Mrs. Henry (Julia) Hanson at Waterton Mills, on the Maskinonge, Waterton Park (Map 6). It was just south of where International Coffee Shop and Cabins were later built. By 1916, A.H. Arthur "Pop" Harwood was appointed mail carrier. Here he is driving "Kate" and "May" hauling the mail from Twin Butte to Waterton Park townsite, where the post office was operated by Jack Hazzard in his hotel (1916-1919). *Author's Collection*

Waterton Oil, Land, & Power Co. sawmill at Waterton Mills, on the shore of Maskinonge Lk, in 1907. Henry Hanson was the proprietor. It was on the east side of the Waterton River, upstream from the future bridge over the river and across from the future Registration Office (Map 6). *Used with the kind permission of The Archives of the Pincher Creek and District Historical Society.*

'Pop' Harwood brought his wife and son, Steve, to Pincher Creek from England in 1905. He had the job of postmaster in Waterton from 1919 – 1950. His first post office was across from Lake Linnet on Lot 9, Block 7.

In the winter of 1920-21, 'Pop' is north of his post office (Map 6).

In 1950, Geordie Annand and I built our family home on the footprint of Pop's post office. The 'old Kootenai Brown' house was on the lot immediately to the south. *Used with the kind permission of The Archives of the Pincher Creek and District Historical Society.*

(Above left) George Baker worked at Oil City in Waterton Park as a young man. In a few years he had saved enough money to buy a Model T truck. He established the Park Transport Company in 1921 in a small building at Park headquarters across from Lake Linnet. Above is the garage he built in the Waterton townsite in 1932 when he greatly expanded his operation.

(Above right) In 1950, Betty Baker (standing, right) poses with Gerald "Slim" Udal (left) and friends by the entrance to the Cameron Lake Store, built by the Bakers in 1939. Betty also rented Cameron Lake Bungalows to tourists and ran a rowboat concession on Cameron Lake, Waterton Park. George and Betty carried on their successful businesses for more than 40 years. *Courtesy Betty Annand Baker*

The Canadian North-West Oil Company drilled for oil at various sites in the Mountain Mill and Beaver Mines area. My grandmother, Alena Munro (Oscar) Vroom owned shares in the company so received a copy of the report of directors to the 3rd Annual General Meeting of Shareholders held in January 1909. The balance sheet dated 31st December, 1908, indicated that the drilling was started in 1905. The report on 'development work' opted for an optimistic tone.

This picture shows the drilling rig at Kelly's Camp in 1927. The camp was located south of Beaver Mines, inside the Castle River Forest Reserve, at the junction of West Castle and Castle Rivers. *Courtesy Katherine Bruce*

This beautiful mounted deer's head is an example of the vocation of taxidermy. In the early 1900s people shot deer mostly for food. However, when a hunter bagged an exceptional specimen, they often had it mounted to tell and retell the story to their children and grandchildren.

Geordie Annand shot this 12-point mule deer buck on the John Wellman ranch just outside the boundary of Waterton Park in 1937. During the Great Depression, deer was a valued source of food when money was very scarce.

This magnificent head still hangs over the fireplace in my daughter Edi-May's home. *Courtesy Edi-May Annand Smithies*

John G. "Kootenai" Brown sits in a car owned by Sarah "Lu" Nielson in front of his home across the road from Lake Linnet, Waterton Park, in 1913 (Map 6). Lu lived in Waterton in the summers but spent the winters in Cardston, AB. While Lu was in Cardston, she and Rose Harker wrote articles for *The Lethbridge Herald*. They also sold subscriptions to the newspaper. For her sales efforts, one year Lu won this Ford as a prize for the most subscriptions sold by anyone. It was the first car in the area. Lu also sold brushes. Her biographers commented, "She was a good business woman." *Courtesy L Pommier*

About 1910, "Sis" Buchanan (Mrs. Charlie Mitchell) stands in front of the office of Dr. Edward Connor in Pincher Creek. Charlie was the brother of my Aunt Ruby (Harold) Vroom. Dad bought Charlie's homestead south of Beaver Mines and it became our home place (Map 2).

Dr. Connor and his wife, Lena, came west in 1910. They moved to Lethbridge in 1916 where he opened the first known clinic and became one of Canada's pre-eminent surgeons. There was no medical or hospital insurance anywhere in Canada until the 1950s. If a loved one was ill for a long period and required medical attention the family would often go into debt to pay the doctor's or hospital bill. Sometimes the doctor (who was usually an independent businessman) would take his fees in 'trade' or farm produce. Or, they accepted no payment at all. *Courtesy R. Jaggernath*

People wanting to start a business in the thriving town of Pincher Creek depended on local tradesmen to construct their buildings. Logan McWhirter, a self-employed carpenter, is shown here on January 16, 1902. Logan (left on the roof) and his crew built the Massey-Harris Co. Ltd. building in 1908-09. Other workers and interested people stand amongst the upright studs of the building. On this day there was a Chinook. The temperature was 49F (10C) in the shade. *Courtesy Essie McWhirter Cox*

My great uncle, Archie Vroom, came west from Nova Scotia in 1903. Details of his working on construction of the CPR through the Crowsnest Pass to Cranbrook are in my book *The Vrooms of the Foothills: Cowboys & Homesteaders.* In 1904, he built the Archie Vroom School on our 'home place' (Map 3). Recognizing an opportunity to become a merchant, Archie went into the dry goods business. He formed a partnership with Mr. Burton and established the Vroom and Burton General Store in Watson, SK. He is seen here with customers and staff in his store in 1908. *Courtesy P, D&A Vroom*

The Jenkins family, who ranched in the Park View district, took a fishing trip into the mountains each fall after the harvest was finished. The weather didn't always co-operate. In the early 1920s, Hez Jenkins (leading) is bringing 10 pack horses, and 2 extra, down a snowy slope on the Middle Kootenay Pass in Waterton Park. *Courtesy B Patriquin*

In the 1920s, 30s and 40s, Robert W. "Bob" Hewitt driving his peddler's wagon was always a welcome sight to farm and ranch families. When he was 12 years, Mr. Hewitt lost one arm in a coal mine accident. But, he was an enterprising soul and became a Watkins Dealer. He worked 30 years as the 'Watkins man' supporting his wife, Selina and two children, Esther and James. Mr. Hewitt covered an area roughly 45 miles square including Pincher Creek, Cowley, Lundbreck, Beaver Mines and Twin Butte. Cash was so scarce during the Great Depression; he once came home after travelling for 2 weeks and had only sold 50¢ worth of goods. Here Bob stands with 'Snip' and 'Tom', h itched to his Bennett buggy, at his home on Bridge Street in Pincher Creek, AB, in 1943. *Courtesy Jim Hewitt*

Henry and Elizabeth Mowat Mitchell at the time of their marriage in 1911. In 1906 Henry hauled incredibly large loads of freight on the 'Oil Trail' from Pincher Station to Oil City by 4- and 8-horse teams. En route they forded Yarrow & Drywood Creeks, crossed the Badlands of Waterton Park, forded Pass Creek near the (later) Canyon Church Camp, drove over the ridge past Blue (Crandell) Lake, and then winched the equipment down the precipitous trail into the Cameron Creek valley. In 1907, Henry was a teamster on a 36-horse team that pulled the huge boiler to Oil City. Elizabeth, a tiny woman who was a tireless worker, died of tuberculosis when their eldest child, Ed, was only 13 years. Henry was left to run the ranch and raise their family. As a girl, Esther Houston (Bodell Horn) remembers that Henry "was doing a great job of raising his family." In 2011, John and Cathy Mitchell and sons are the fifth generation to live on and work the Mitchell ranch in the Parkview district. *Courtesy B Mitchell Skinner*

PASSIONS

Homesteaders and settlers in western Canada came from varied backgrounds. Once here they occasionally found they had time on their hands. Many, if not most, people developed a passion of some kind. A passion in the context of this book is any long-tem project or ongoing activity in which someone is keenly interested. The project may or may not be financially rewarding, but it is always personally rewarding. Pursuing one's passion makes what might otherwise be a rather humdrum life worthwhile and even exciting. Some of the passions pursued by homesteaders and settlers in SW Alberta include: photography recording everyday happenings and the magnificent scenery, hand-painted murals on log cabin walls, wool embroidery on gunny sacking, reading and chasing wild horses.

This is my dad, Ralph Vroom, at his campsite in the East Kootenays in 1918. Dad had many passions. However, I think he was the most passionate about living the free life of a cowboy. In the summer of 1918 he indulged that passion by chasing wild horses in the East Kootenays of BC. He holds two wild horses that he would tame and sell to make extra cash. The saddle horses he used for the chase are on the right of the tent.

A few years later Dad chased wild horses in the mountainous area surrounding the Arrow Lakes in BC. There he met Ira Lum. (See Dad's picture with Ira and John Barrymore in Chapter 4.) For years Dad told enthralling stories of his adventures. He used the Middle Kootenay Pass when he was riding from Beaver Creek valley to the Flathead River country in southeast BC to hunt wild horses. *Author's Collection*

About 1920, my mom, Mollie Tyson Vroom, sits beside a simple bouquet of garden flowers. She is wearing a dress trimmed with a white crocheted collar.

Mom loved to knit and crochet. She did a number of pieces before her hands became very severely inflamed with rheumatoid arthritis. When she could no longer do fine crocheting, Mom continued to do home-sewing, making dresses for herself and coats and dresses for my sister, Marion, and me. Even then, Mom continued crocheting wool tops for the felt-soled slippers she had to wear on her painful, arthritic feet instead of regular shoes. *Author's Collection*

My grandmother E. Mary Tyson grew up in Scotland and lived in the Lake District of England before immigrating to Canada with her husband, George, and children, Tommy and Mollie, in 1914. Granny loved all things that had to do with the out-of-doors - walking, gardening, fishing, and picnicking. However, I think that fishing was Granny's passion. Often on summer's day Granny took her fishing rod and walked to the Waterton River about one-half mile east of their farm at Fishburn. There she fished until she had a string of whitefish, which were delicious when fried in hot butter for dinner. *Courtesy G&S Tyson*

Geordie Annand's great passion was fishing, often for bull trout in Pass Creek, Waterton Park, as here in 1948. He usually caught his limit. This bridge was built in 1918 to replace a snow-collapsed bridge on the historic Oil Trail (Map 6) from Pincher Creek to Oil City. In the early 1900s, this was the route along which Foxy McKenzie, Henry Mitchell and others freighted materials, supplies and mail during the oil 'boom' years. Mount Blakiston, distant background, shows beautifully against a clear blue sky. *Author's Collection*

My grandfather George Tyson was a very quiet man with a droll sense of humour. His passion when he was a young man was looking after the horse that he drove, as seen here, on the mail cart between Ambleside and Consiton, in the Lakes District, Eng. He, Granny and family immigrated to Canada in 1914. When he was older, he read the newspaper regularly and followed the news on the radio. During the many years that he farmed in the Fishburn, district my grandfather did not own a tractor. He did all the farm work using his faithful team of horses. *Author's Collection*

Riding horseback was my main passion from the time I was three years old until my late teens. I rode four and one-half miles to school and back for seven years. During the War Years, my brother Don and I rented saddle horses at Red Rock Canyon in Waterton Park and at the Canadian Air Force (RCAF) base at Claresholm. When I was attending Pincher Creek High School, we often spent weekends getting some of Dad's horses out of the pound in Pincher Creek and taking them back to the range at Beaver Mines. Here, in 1943, I am standing beside my gentle saddle horse named "Whip." I am dressed in jodhpurs and riding boots. The padded lady's saddle once belonged to my grandmother Alena Munro Vroom. I am at the back door of the Pincher Creek house that Mom, Don, Bill, Marion and I were living in at the time. Dad was Overseas in the Canadian Army for five years during WWII. *Author's Collection*

Over the years my passions evolved to homemaking, child rearing, church and community volunteer work, going back teaching elementary school children, completing my Bachelor of Education degree and attaining my Master of Education degree, specializing in the teaching of reading. I taught until I retired. Now my passion is writing social history books. Left to right: Bessie Vroom Ellis, Vera Cyr Gingras, Edi-May Annand Smithies, Margerie Warren Shenton. Photo taken when I gave an 'Author's Talk' at the Pincher Creek Library in September 2010. *Author's Collection*

Sarah McJanet (George) Ballantyne had a lively wit. In about 1928, she poses with a twinkle in her eye in the house yard of Ballantyne's Store and Post Office, Beaver Mines. (Map 1) She is wearing a stylish winter coat with a black fox fur collar. Mrs. Ballantyne made all of the dresses, coats and blouses worn by her daughters, Elva and Alma "Jo".

She trained as a seamstress in eastern Canada, going from home to home staying with each family until she completed their season's clothes. She used a hand-operated, portable sewing machine.

In 2011, Ryan and Jessica McClelland, son and daughter-in-law of Doug and Lee Gingras McClelland, and their family still live on the original Ballantyne farmstead east of Beaver Mines. Ryan is the great grandson of George and Sarah Ballantyne. . *Courtesy Alma "Jo" Johnson*

This elegant, hand-operated, portable sewing machine was brought from England to Pincher Creek by Margaret Hingley (Mrs. Harry) Clements when she immigrated. She made the clothes of her daughter, Marjory Clements (David Link) who later was one of my favourite teachers.

Similar machines were used by almost every other homemaker in the countryside for sewing clothing their families, which was a passion for many. *Courtesy Ginger Link Reimer*

Mrs. Etta B Platt (left), a resident of Waterton Park for many years, and a friend playing guitars and singing harmony in about 1940. Mrs. Platt was a long-time friend of my parents, Ralph and Mollie Tyson Vroom. Mrs. Platt had many passions. She attended Waterton community functions, entertaining the crowd with her singing and sense of humour. Mrs. Platt also made western clothing, hand-decorating them with wool embroidery

This photo is one of many that my Dad carried with him when he was Overseas in WWII, to remind him of his family and friends 'back home.' *Author's Collection*

In the 1920s and 30s, house parties were the most common form of entertainment. Families were larger then than now so there was always an audience or dance partner. In 1922, Dewey Truitt (left) holds his guitar. His brother, Lawrence, holds his violin. All the boys in John and Melcina Truitt's family played violin. They are in front of their home on the family farm in Pleasant (Gladstone) Valley.

Amateur musicians, such as these two young men, often played impromptu concerts for friends and neighbours or provided dance music at house parties throughout the district. Regular passionate, joyous practice brings out the best in all musicians. *Courtesy Adam & Hazel Truitt*

In 1934, the Good Companions Orchestra (left to right) Bob Coulthart, piano accordion; Mr. Hollenback, drums; Michael Bruce, banjo, at the Bruce home, Beaver Mines. They used their gift to earn a few extra dollars during the Depression playing at house parties and dances, such as the 1934 New Year's Eve party of the Beaver Mines Women's Institute (admission 25 cents). *Courtesy Katherine Bruce*

Children could spend hours fishing in a creek near their home. It didn't matter whether they caught fish. Just the joy of being outdoors on their own was enough. About 1917, the sons of Mabel and Edward Bruce (left to right) Ronald, Michael and Anthony, sit on a log across Mill Creek with their fishing lines dangling (Map 7). They lived nearby at the 'old' Roodee ranch, on the north bank of the Castle River, where Robert 'Chappy' & Elizabeth Clarkson once had a polo ground. A few years later fishing and hunting had become a passion for the boys. They got dinner for the family many times. *Courtesy K Bruce*

Peigan Indians in full costume dress in 1928. (Left to right) Chief Philip Big Swan, Chief Johnny Crow Eagle, Jack Crowshoe and Chickee. The men are about to perform in the Sun Dance on the Brocket reserve east of Pincher Creek. *Courtesy N. Brister*

In the early days of motor travel, people loved to have their picture taken just sitting in one of the new, horseless carriages. In 1913, Kootenai Brown and his wife Nichemoos sit in the (centre) back seat of Sarah 'Lu' Nielson's Ford, the first car in the Waterton Park area. Lu was a generous soul; she likely took them for a 'spin' occasionally. *Author's Collection*

Jim Sr. and Veralyn English frequently brought their family to Waterton Park to visit Jim's parents, Joe and Emma. About 1955, back row (left to right) Jim English, Sr., Joe and Emma; front row, Jimmy and Jaycee English. Jim Sr. went fishing on Waterton Lakes with his dad. Jimmy and Jaycee played with the neighbourhood children, those of Geordie and Bessie Annand, and Jack and Effie Christiansen. Jimmy English spent several summers with his grandparents. This house, across the road from Lake Linnet, was built in 1920 by John T. "Jack" Gladstone, son of William "Old Glad" Gladstone. *Courtesy Jim English*

Annie Hescott (married Emil Jack in 1911) was raised in the Spread Eagle district north of Waterton Park. She was passionate about photography. Like Etta McRae and Connie Holroyd, Annie developed her own photos. The Hescott family travelled by team and wagon to go camping in Waterton Park every summer. On the right-hand side of this photo, taken by Annie, are their family's tents on the lakeshore of Upper Waterton Lake. In 1911, this became the site of the Jack Hazzard Hotel on Main Street. In 1927, the Prince of Wales Hotel was built on the hill seen in the background (left). *Courtesy E Jack Hochstein*

Connie Warburton (Mrs. John C. "Bo") Holroyd stands at the old Forks cabin, the original warden's cabin at Red Rock Canyon in Waterton Park in 1924. This cabin was located on a bench just west of the confluence of Pass Creek and Red Rock Creek. Connie, who trained as a nurse in Prince Edward Island, was passionate about her life as a warden's wife. She also spent many hours helping neighbours when people were ill. Connie was very artistic. She developed and printed her own photos and painted. A large picture of a mountain goat, charcoal on canvas, hung for many years on the front of this cabin, protected by the overhang. *Courtesy Jack Holroyd*

(Left to right) Ronald, Michael and Anthony Bruce. In his memoirs, Anthony explained that, as there was no Boy Scout Troop at Beaver Mines, the three Bruce boys formed a Wolf Patrol. Boys in a Wolf Patrol worked on their own with help from their parents. The brothers hiked all over the Beaver Mines countryside. They climbed mountains and observed wildlife of all sorts. Michael recorded many of their exploits with his camera, a "vest pocket Kodak; Model B." He took 40 rolls of film in 1927-1928 alone. *Courtesy K Bruce*

In 1961, Waterton Park Brownies enjoy a social evening at the cabin of the Lewiston, MT, Girl Scouts. (Left to right) Debbie Camp, Mary Ann Haug, Maureen Vance, Mary Lee Schmidt, Sheila Ross, Karma Vance, Susie Camp, Ellen McCallum.

The Girl Scouts were in Waterton on a week-long field trip. Waterton Park Brown Owl at that time was Jean (Mrs. Bert) Murray. Girl Guiding and Boy Scouting were a passion for many. *Author's Collection*

A group of Pincher Creek cadets stand at ease in 1925, east of the newly built Pincher Creek United Church. In the foreground are Henry (surname unknown), left, and Sydney Baker, right. Sydney's mother was postmistress in Pincher Creek at the time. This picture was taken looking west. *Courtesy Kay Leigh*

My younger sister, Marion Vroom (Mike Grechman), is skiing on a gentle slope on Dad and Mom's ranch south of Beaver Mines in 1946 (Map 4). She is eight years old. Marion practiced diligently, gradually skiing down bigger hills.

She became a very good skier by her teens. In 1951-1952, Marion lived with Geordie and me across from Lake Linnet. She attended Waterton Park School. By then, she was skiing down a hill in Waterton known as "Suicide Run," on the bottom few hundred yards of Bertha Mountain. *Author's collection*

Every summer for about 10 years Mr. and Mrs. Don Gannon from Regina and their daughters came to Waterton Park for a 10-day vacation. They stayed in Vimyvue Cabins, owned by George and Betsy Annand because the cabin had a cook stove which still used wood for fuel. When Vimyvue modernized and put in propane gas cooking ranges, the Gannons instead stayed in the Cameron Lake Bungalows which still use wood for fuel. Here in about 1964 are (left to right) Evelyn and David Annand and Patti Gannon swimming in the frigid waters of 'Cleopatra's Bathtub' in Red Rock Canyon Creek. *Courtesy P Gannon Wellings*

During the 1930s, the only swimming pools were deep pools of water in local creeks and streams. The swift current of a river formed dangerous whirlpools. Dams built by a colony of beavers in many local creeks provided pools that were deep enough for an adult to swim in. Here six lovely women from the McIvor family enjoy a relaxing afternoon at their favourite swimming hole. The father of Jane McIvor Rutledge was a good friend of my Dad's. *Courtesy Jean Burns*

Most boys that I knew as a child could climb trees. Very few of the girls could climb a tree. However, Barbara "Billie" or "Barbwire" Prigge was an exception. In about 1928, Billie sits comfortably on the limb of a tall spruce tree. The limbs of this tree are evenly spaced so that they provide a stairway leading to the top of the tree.

Billie's father, Reginald (Alice) was the forest ranger at Mill Creek Ranger Station (south end of Gladstone Valley) from 1920-1934 (Map 3). He was stationed at Elk Lodge Ranger Station (south end of Beaver Creek valley) from 1934–1936. Both Mill Creek and Elk Lodge cabins were built in 1920, when they were warden cabins within Waterton Lakes National Park. From 1914-1921, the Park extended from the 49th parallel to the Carbondale River. *Courtesy K Bruce*

Water skiing on Middle Waterton Lake was a passion of many. Park headquarters are in the upper background in 1950. Homes (left to right): the 'old' Kootenai Brown house; Geordie and Bessie Annand, under construction (Map 6); 'Lochvue' of George and Betsy Annand; Vimyvue, a duplex owned by the Annands; Joe and Emma English home, and after 1952,

Simmons Moegenson. *Author's Collection*

The settlers' passion for picnicking carried on to succeeding generations. In 1962, our family enjoys a lunch in the shade 'down the river' in Waterton Park. (Left to right) Edi-May, Bessie, James, Geordie and Evelyn. Our son Dave took the photo. Both Geordie and I were descendants of homesteaders in the southwest corner of Alberta. My friend, Robin LaGrandeur, remembers that after it had rained and haying was delayed on the McLaughlin ranch east of Pincher Creek, it was "make up a lunch and head for the river bottom for a picnic." *Author's Collection.*

Travelling to the eastern seaboard of the US from Waterton Park in 1948 required a lot of planning and a good deal of enthusiasm or passion. Prior to the trip, George and Betsy Annand bought a new Chevrolet car from their son-in-law, George Baker of Park Transport Company, Waterton. This is a reunion of the Annand brothers and sisters who had emigrated from Scotland. (Left to right) unknown, Betsy (George) Annand, George Annand, Elizabeth Annand Wilkins, James Wilkins, Jean Stewart (Will) Annand, Will Annand, Susan Hanshumaker (Dave) Annand, Dave Annand. *Author's Collection*

LOVE THY NEIGHBOUR

In the early part of the twentieth century communities were held together by various organizations and family celebrations that took people outside of themselves and their own lives. Churches of many denominations were built by the early settlers. These churches became rallying points in the sustaining of homesteaders and settlers in southwest Alberta.

These hardy people also joined forces to construct buildings that would benefit the whole community. Youth groups gave feelings of self worth and pride in individual and group achievement to the youth of isolated communities. Informal community groups raised money to help furnish halls; churches brought the organizational skills of men and women to the fore. Special family celebrations brought people together. The generosity and empathy of neighbours in a particularly stressful situation helped to forge friendships that lasted a lifetime.

I'm 17 years old in 1944 and a student at Pincher Creek High School. I picked the bouquet of flowers while on a hike up to "the canyon." The canyon was a popular recreation area along Pincher Creek about a mile west of town.

I wore a similar outfit while out hunting horses in the Twin Butte area one spring weekend. I was riding a 'snakey' horse, and the seam of my pants split. Olive Bonertz recalls there was a dance at the Twin Butte Community Hall, but girls were not allowed to wear pants and I didn't have a skirt. Olive asked the dance chaperones, Mr. Cox and Mrs. Dora (Bill) Terrill, if I could wear her riding pants. In a great act of kindness to a teenager, they allowed me to wear Olive's riding pants at the dance. I became the first girl to wear pants to a dance at Twin Butte Community Hall.

Once when riding from our ranch (Map 4) at Beaver Mines, I got tangled up in some beaver dams northwest of Twin Butte. The further I went into the water-soaked area, the more serious trouble I was in. I was saved when Ralph Gold, a local rancher and a long-time friend of Dad's, happened along and led me out. *Author's Collection*

In September, 1941, at Kingston, ON are brothers Alfred, left, and Ralph Vroom, right. When soldiers signed up for service to their country, they often didn't even know where or when they would be sent Overseas. Even today, soldiers' families make do as best they can while soldiers are serving their country for the good of all of us.

In the fall of 1916, Alfred was newly married to Margaret Coulter of Hillcrest, AB. Margaret didn't know Alfred had been sent Overseas until she got a card from Moose Jaw saying he and his brother, Harold, were on the train across Canada. In November 1916, Harold and Alfred arrived in England together on the Empress of Britain. They were both sent to France with 192nd Battalion. My dad, Ralph, was married with four children when he served Overseas for 5 years in WWII. *Author's collection*

At least five teams of horses and six men are moving this house up the east side of Mill Creek Valley. It was a community effort. This is Ann Harley Link's house being moved in about 1920 to the Link ranch, prior to the Link family moving to the McLaren ranch at Mountain Mill in the spring of 1924 (Map 7). Her house was originally located on the west side of the Castle River, before the river goes under the bridge. The house became a granary and was still in use in 2006. *Courtesy K. Bruce*

Local women acting as midwives were a vital part of the healthy survival of mothers and their newborns. Often women, such as Agatha Fitzgerald (John A.) Drader, lived in very isolated places.

In a letter written to me by Ernest S. Drader , of Cutbank, MT, in 1963, Ernest explained that *Chee-pay-qua-ka-soo* or 'Blue Flash-of-Lightning', also known as 'Nichemoos', wife of John G. 'Kootenai' Brown, was the midwife for his mother when Ernest was born at Oil City, Waterton Park, AB, on December 26, 1906.

Nichemoos was also Ernest's godmother when he was baptized in Pincher Creek by Father Lacombe, early in 1907. *Galt Museum and Archives P19760230113*

The Emile and Elise Gingras family. (Left to right) Back: Elise, Sister Juliet, Emile, Gerald, Homer, Adrian; Middle: Helen and Maurice; Front: Jean. Sister Juliet, who devoted her life to good works, joined a Roman Catholic Order. She was the sister-in-law of my cousin, Vera (Mrs. Homer) Cyr Gingras. *Courtesy Elva Ballantyne McClelland*

The O'Neill family, in Ottawa, ON, January 1928, at Michael's ordination as a Roman Catholic priest. (Left to right): Hugh, Mary, Michael, Maude, William and Evelyn. Michael stands beside his mother, Maude Vroom O'Neill, sister of my grandfather Oscar. Years later, when Michael became Archbishop of the Regina Diocese of the Roman Catholic Church, Dad and Mom travelled to Regina, SK, to attend the ceremony. *Author's Collection*

(Left) Nellie Gladstone ('Frenchy') Riviere and Isabella 'Nichemoos' (Kootenai Brown) sit on the steps of Nellie's home west of Twin Butte in 1929 (Map 4). As there were no senior citizens' homes, elders were cared for by family or friends. Nellie was very good to Nichemoos. *Courtesy F Riviere McWhirter*

Marjorie Haugen (left) of Cowley, AB, and Jean Burns of Pincher Creek were two people honoured for their lifelong service to their communities during celebrations held to commemorate the Golden Jubilee (1952-1972) of Queen Elizabeth II. They received a "lifetime of giving" award from David Coutts, MLA for Livingstone-Macleod, at a special event in the Pincher Creek Senior Centre. Mrs. Haugen taught school in Pincher Creek for 26 years, including two years in a one-room school north of Cowley. Mrs. Burns and her husband, Vern, owned and operated a men's clothing store in Pincher Creek for many years. *Courtesy Adeline Cyr Robbins*

Offerings of fruit and vegetables fill the back pew of Fishburn Church Thanksgiving Day, 1940. Gerry Hutchinson was the minister. Thanksgiving has been celebrated in the Fishburn Church for more than 100 years. The church was built by volunteers and is lovingly maintained by descendants of those builders. Student ministers conduct services during the summer months. The rest of the year, the minister is shared with another church. *Courtesy Bessie Thomas Halton*

When summer ministers started coming to the Fishburn area in 1904, parishioners travelled to church by team and wagon or democrat. Due to the isolation of many families, it was also important that the church go to the people.

Harley Richmond was one of the summer ministers who held services at various places in the Fishburn area. Here he stands on the prairie near Marr School (Map 5) where he held occasional church services. The summer minister boarded with various families. *Courtesy Gladys Cummins*

St. Henry's Roman Catholic Church sits proudly atop a rise in the Yarrow district about 18 miles southeast of Pincher Creek (Map 5). Like other small churches in southwest Alberta, it was built by people who homesteaded in the area. St. Henry's is cared for by parishioners and their families who have attended it over the years. The church is cleaned by the women of the parish. The men organize work parties and do regular maintenance of the church. *Courtesy Edith Jack Hochstein*

Two ranchers' wives sit visiting while attending the Sun Dance ceremony at the Peigan Indian Reserve, Brocket, AB, in the 1930s.

From the time the first Europeans travelled to the western plains of Canada, those who showed kindness to the native people were welcomed. Newcomers were generously invited by the people of nearby Indian Reserves to attend important celebrations, such as the Sun Dance. Visitors packed picnic lunches and made a day-long trip of the occasion. *Courtesy Katherine Bruce*

Members of the congregation of Mountain Mill Church stand around exchanging the news of the day with their neighbours (Map 7). By 1922, some people were driving motor vehicles to church rather than travelling with a team and wagon or democrat. Some of the men are eyeing their neighbours' cars with great interest. The girl on the right is Alma "Jo" Ballantyne (Johnson).

     Mountain Mill Church was dedicated in June 1906. Pictures and stories of the 100th anniversary celebrations of the church are in my book, *The Vrooms of the Foothills: Cowboys and Homesteaders. Courtesy Alma "Jo" Ballantyne Johnson*

September 11, 1938, Christening Day for Malcolm "Mel" Leigh. (Left to right) Charlie Joyce, Ada Kembell (holding Malcolm) and Ben Hardy. Charlie was first godfather; Ben was second godfather; Ada was godmother and had the honour of holding baby Malcolm to have his picture taken. It was a big responsibility to assume the role of a godparent, to take over raising the child if the parent couldn't. The whole community rejoiced with the family on the day of a baby's christening. *Courtesy K Leigh*

All Saints Anglican Church, Waterton Park, in the 1930s. Canon Samuel H. Middleton prevailed upon Louis Hill of the Great Northern Railway to make a substantial donation to finance the church. It was built by Oland Construction of Lethbridge for the Anglican Diocese of Calgary in 1928.

My older daughter, Edi-May, and I were both married in All Saints. Geordie Annand and I were married on September 11, 1948. Our children, Edi-May, Evelyn, David and James, were baptized in the church. Edi-May married Wayne Smithies of Kingston, ON, on August 28, 1971. *Courtesy Gavin MacKay*

Gerry and Nellie Hunter Goble Hadfield, along with little Linda, moved out of most of their house during the tourist season and rented it out to visitors to Waterton Park. On September 11, 1948, the main part of the house accommodated Geordie's and my wedding reception guests. It was a very generous gesture of Nellie and Gerry. Nellie also instructed me in making cakes and cookies – she let me bake a lot of cookies! They were served at our reception.

My bridesmaids were Nan Delaney (John Dexter "Decker" Stewart), Waterton and Shirley (Irvin Morton), Milk River, AB. Robina Hewitt Peterson of Hesketh, AB, was my matron-of-honour. Frank Goble was our groomsman. Photo by Frank Goble. *Courtesy F Goble*

A joyous family Christmas 1945, on our ranch south of Beaver Mines (Map 2). (Left to right) Mollie, Ralph, Bessie, Bill, Don, Marion and "Tippy." This was the first time our family was together in four years.

Dad was in the Army, and Overseas, most of those years. Our ranch was rented. Mom and we children lived mainly in Pincher Creek where we attended school. On weekends Don and I looked after our herd of saddle horses as best we could. During summer holidays we rented saddle horses, first at Red Rock Canyon, then at the Claresholm RCAF station. By the time Dad came home I was teaching school near Drumheller; Don was just ready to leave home to seek work in BC; my brother, Bill, and my sister, Marion, were still in public school. *Courtesy Don Vroom*

Geordie and Bessie Annand's home in Waterton Park under construction in 1950 (Map 6). I drew the design and a Lethbridge architect drew up the plans. Carl Carlson oversaw pouring the basement walls. Howie Millham from Taber, AB, supervised the framing of the walls and roof. Our home was built across the road from Lake Linnet, on the footprint of A.H. "Pop" Harwood's post office which had burned in 1930. Generous friends, who were Park employees, are spending their Sunday off closing in the roof. Geordie, his dad George and I did most of the interior finishing – a lot of sweat equity!

The house partially visible at front left is the 'old' Kootenai Brown house. In 1913, Kootenai moved into this house from his homestead so, as Superintendent in all but official title, he could be nearer where tourists camped across the road on Aldridge Bay, Middle Waterton Lake. *Author's Collection*

All Saints Anglican Church annual Sunday school picnic, 1944, at J.C. "Bo" and Connie Holroyd's home, "Cedar Cabin" warden station on Knight's Lake (Map 6).

Standing far left, Mrs. Gerry Bailey, whose husband ran the fish hatchery. Mrs. Helen (Percy) Gregory was the Sunday school superintendent for a number of years. Here, wearing a sweater and leaning over the table, she helps serve food to a group of hungry children. Directly behind Mrs. Gregory is Effie Barnes Black, daughter of long-time Waterton warden, Bert Barnes. The dog is "Terry," self-appointed guardian of 2-year-old Alice Holroyd. *Courtesy E Hamilton*

Meeting of the Waterton Ladies Sewing Circle, 1933, in the front yard of George and Betty Annand Baker home on Evergreen Ave. (Clockwise left to right) Mrs. Arletta "Lettie" (Oliver) Goble (far left in knitted white hat), Annie Eddy (Gene Morris), Mrs. Agnes (Cpl. Andy) Ford, unknown (black fur collar), Inez (Andy) Stratton (standing), Mrs. Arthur H. "Pop" Harwood (standing), unknown (seated), Mrs. Hannah Carnell Presley (adjusting her glasses), Mrs. Jean Clark (Hugh) Galbraith, Mrs. Olga Lund (Eric) Hagglund (partially obscured in striped coat), Mrs. Nellie Hunter (Ed) Goble (seated, turning to face camera; later Mrs. Gerry Hadfield), Mrs. Christine "Chrissie" (Ralph M. "Chris") Christiansen (back to camera). The women met regularly to raise money for various community projects. Photo by Frank Goble. *Courtesy F&L Goble*

In 1929, George R. Annand, Sr., stands behind his 1927 Chevrolet coupe. 'Sport,' his beloved German shepherd, clambers out of the rumble seat. George was an active volunteer in the Waterton community. He was the first Chairman of the Waterton School Board from 1925-1929. He and Betsy's children, Betty and George Jr. "Geordie" attended the school. George was president of the Waterton War Activities committee from 1941-1944, raising funds for soldiers Overseas in WWII. The Annands operated a dairy in Waterton Park from 1920-1926. He was the first man hired when Oland Construction began building the Prince of Wales Hotel. George was storekeeper for the Dept. of Mines and Resources in Waterton from 1929-1951. *Author's Collection*

Like her father, Betty Annand (George) Baker was a tireless community worker. She donated the baptismal font for the Waterton Park United Church. She was awarded a plaque for "Citizen of the Year, Waterton Park" in 1982. Family and friends gathered in Waterton cemetery, April 27, 2006. Fondly remembering her are (left to right) Back row: James "Jim" Annand, Bob Brown (partial), Scott Baker, unknown (sunglasses), Rick Baker, unknown (partial), Bradley Riehl, Holly Vaselenek, Cole Baker, Brian Baker, Rob and Penny Baker, Rae Baker, Mark Baker, Penny Baker, Steve & Robinn Jordan, Bryan Morgan; Middle row: Megan Lailey, Evelyn Annand Lailey, Rev. Joyce Sasse (United Church minister), Edi-May Annand Smithies, Dwayne Nieboer (hand on shoulder of Carla Baker Nieboer); Seated: Carla Baker, Barbara Baker Brown, Cathy Baker, Shari Baker Morgan. *Courtesy Edi-May Smithies*

During WWII, Waterton Park residents raised a considerable sum of money to give financial assistance to local men and women who were Overseas. For one fund raiser, Chief Warden J.C. "Bo" Holroyd donated a saddle horse as a raffle prize. Bo thought the Waterton Park beer parlour would be a good place to sell some tickets. He led the horse up to the bar room door and went inside to drum up some interest.

The horse didn't stand placidly outside, however. It had other ideas. The horse walked into the bar room and joined the Saturday night crowd. The bartenders were alarmed, but the beer drinkers loved it. The tickets "sold like hotcakes," recalled Jack, Bo's younger son.

This picture shows a congenial Bo Holroyd in the 1960s. *Courtesy Jack Holroyd*

Harold and Gada Bruns, at their 70th Wedding Anniversary party, were married in the 1930s. At that time, Harold was pitching bundles on a farm in the Pincher Creek area. They met at a party in the district. When I met them, Gada was matron of the Pincher Creek High School dormitory where I boarded. Harold drove the school bus from Brocket to Pincher Creek. They were extremely kind to all young people over the years. *Courtesy H&G Bruns*

My cousin, Adeline Cyr Robbins (right) and I at Crestview Lodge On the bed are examples of handiwork, preserving, baking and sewing items Adeline entered in the Pincher Creek and District Fair in 2004. She started entering soon after she graduated from the Olds School of Agriculture in Olds, AB, in the 1920s and continued for 60 years. *Author's Collection*

Funeral procession of William Shanks "Old Glad" Gladstone along Main Street in Pincher Creek, AB, on April 11, 1911. *The Lethbridge Daily Herald,* April 12, 1911, carried a front-page account with details of the funeral service. Pallbearers were C. (Charles) Kettles, W.S. (William) Lees, A. (Andrew) Christie, P. (Peter) McIlquiham and A.E. (Arthur) Cox. The funeral was conducted by the Old Timers' Association and took place in Scott's undertaking parlour. Three Protestant ministers took part in the funeral service. Interment was in the Episcopal cemetery.

"Old Glad" was an apprentice with the Hudson's Bay Company when he came west in 1869. He helped build Fort Macleod and the sawmill at Mountain Mill. He and his wife, Harriett, took out a homestead at Mountain Mill. They raised their family there. He donated some of his homestead land for the Mountain Mill Church. At his death he was the oldest old-timer in the district. A loaded packhorse (far left), symbolic of Old Glad's younger years, was led behind a democrat in the procession. *Courtesy Hugh Dempsey*

Cecilie "Squish" Swanson Parke of Pincher Creek and Waterton Park (left) and Bessie Ellis at her 90th birthday party. Dr. Brian 'Barney' and Mary Ann Healey Reeves hosted the party at their home 'Trail's End', Waterton, June 2010.

Archdeacon Cecil (Enid) "Swanny" Swanson, Squish's father, was instrumental in establishing All Saints Anglican Church, Waterton. Squish and her father attended the coronation of Queen Elizabeth II in 1953. Her father was awarded the Order of Canada for his work with the Anglican Church. Squish still takes an active interest in looking after All Saints Church. *Author's Collection*

In 1950, Morning Bull, a well known leader of the Peigan Indian band at Brocket, AB, is with a number of oldtimers from the Pincher Creek area. (Left to right) Back row: Bill Tourond, Sr., Nahor Dilatush, Percy Stuckey, Sam Stuckey, Mr. Hughes; Middle row: Harry Gunn, Mrs. A. Kubasek, Mrs. McDonnell, Mrs. Phil Grey, Mrs. C. Kemble, Mrs. Fred Schoening, Mrs. Elisa Sorge, James Taylor, Mrs. Callahan, William Foote, Robert Lang; Front row: George Pelletier, Morning Bull, Adam L. "Scotty" Freebairn, Joe Fournier, Mrs. Morning Bull, unknown.

When he died at 92 years, Chief Morning Bull was given a traditional funeral. In a ceremonial parade along Main Street, Pincher Creek, Morning Bull's saddle horse carrying an empty saddle was led behind the casket. His obituary appeared in the Pincher Creek Echo, March 3, 1992. *Photo of Pincher Creek Oldtimers on Main Street, 1950, as found in "Pincher Creek Memories", Pincher Creek: Republished by the Pincher Creek and District Historical Society, 1975, p. 53.*

In 2010, Bessie Ellis at her home in Victoria wearing the Commemorative Medal she was awarded in 1992 marking the 125th Anniversary of Canada. The certificate that Bessie received with the medal states: "The Commemorative Medal for the 125th Anniversary of the Confederation of Canada is conferred upon Mrs. Bessie Ellis in recognition of significant contribution to compatriots, community and to Canada". It is signed by R. J. Hnatychyn, Governor General of Canada.

These medals were given to 125 people in each federal riding in Canada. It is to be worn only at certain ceremonial events, for example, Remembrance Day ceremonies or a church service marking the Battle of the Atlantic. Photo by Mandy Annand. *Author's Collection*

On December 31, 2002, Bessie's family gathered in Victoria, BC, to celebrate her 75th birthday. (Left to right) Back row: Edi-May Annand Smithies, Wayne Smithies, Evelyn Annand Lailey, Michael Lailey, Shelley McConnell, James W. "Jim" Annand, Vanessa Annand, David Annand, Mandy Annand, Shaylah Annand; In front of the back row: Warren Smithies, Megan Lailey, Gerry Hoff Annand, Genevieve Annand; Seated on chesterfield: my brother Donald Vroom and his wife Doreen Lund Vroom, Joseph Meade, Bessie Vroom Ellis; Seated on floor: Eric Lailey, "Rookie," Jay Annand.

My books ensure that my stories and photos, as well as the memories and pictures of many other friends and family will be handed down to succeeding generations. *Author's collection*

My newest grandchild, Declan, was born September 2008. Here in October 2010, Declan, dressed as a railway engineer and sitting in the cab of Thomas the Tank Engine, heads out to go 'trick or treating.' Dressing up in a costume, and pretending to be someone you are not, is an old Hallowe'en tradition in Canada.

Declan will bring joy to the neighbours' hearts. Declan's parents, Jim and Shelley McConnell Annand, made Declan's costume by using odd pieces of plumbing parts and other items that were around the house and amongst Jim's plumbing supplies. *Courtesy Shelley McConnell & Jim Annand*

EPILOGUE

This is the third volume of a multi-volume social history series that I am writing. It contains over 270 pictures illustrating the many different ways in which people made a living in the late 19th and early to mid 20th centuries. The pictures are from the collections of people who are descendants of pioneers and homesteaders in southwestern Alberta. There are 7 maps that show the location of various mines, rivers and homesteads. They built roads and bridges to access the surface and underground wealth found in this vast country. They built new homes to replace log and sod cabins and developed a system of country schools to ensure the education of their children. As well, this book tells of the fun families had at their social events. .

My first two books, *The VROOMS of the FOOTHILLS, Volume 1: Adventures of my Childhood*, 2006, and *The VROOMS of the FOOTHILLS, Volume 2: Cowboys & Homesteaders*, 2008, are available from Trafford Publishing at www.trafford.com and at bookstores in Claresholm, Fort Macleod, Beaver Mines, Pincher Creek, Twin Butte and Waterton Park, AB.

Volume 1: Adventures of My Childhood tells about my life as a young child living on a remote ranch in the Alberta foothills southwest of Pincher Creek. It relates how and why I learned to ride a horse by myself when I was less than three years old and about some of my other experiences and adventures. My most exciting adventure, which happened when I was 10 years old, was going with my Dad when he trapped and shot a grizzly bear deep in the Rocky Mountains.

Volume 2: Cowboys & Homesteaders covers the era from 1884 to 1914 when cowboys, settlers and homesteaders poured into western Canada. It is illustrated with over 220 picture and seven original maps.

My next book is *The VROOMS of the FOOTHLLS, Volume 4: Ranching, the Real West*. It will have over 200 pictures. The picture captions will be historical vignettes. As well as the actual work of ranching, *The Vrooms of the Foothills, Volume 4: Ranching the Real West*, will show ranchers doing other jobs to make a living and to keep their homesteads going. For example, my parents, Ralph and Mollie Tyson Vroom, ran a lumber camp near Paulson, BC. As well, some men who started out as homesteaders became Park and game wardens.

Many homesteaders and/or their sons and daughters enlisted in the Boer War, WWI, WWII and other wars. When they went Overseas, some of them left behind half-grown families. The families adapted because they had to. For example, in our family we had a lot of fun renting saddle horses to tourists at Red Rock Canyon in Waterton Lakes National Park in the summer time to earn extra money for our schooling while Dad was Overseas. Some Canadian servicemen married young women in England, Holland, and other parts of the world and brought them home to Canada. This added to the cultural diversity that makes Canada one of the most desirable countries in the world in which to live.

Illustration courtesy of Trudy Cox Handl

Some members of the Beaver Mines Women's Institute in 1923 (named left to right). Back row: unknown, Alena Munro (Mrs. Oscar) Vroom, Olga Lund (Mrs. Erik) Hagglund looking down, Petrena Aure (Mrs. Peter) Kyllo partially obscured, Jessie Wilger (Rev. Gavin) Hamilton, white hair; Edna (Mrs Mickey) McDonald; unknown obscured.

2nd row from back: Bessie Norton (Mrs. Robert) Lang in front of Alena, Jessie (Mrs. Rev. Gavin) Hamilton, Emma Price (Mrs. William D. "W.D.") McDowall, Miss Tilley (from Alberta Department of Extension), Elsie Belle Crosbie (Mrs. Edward) Joyce, bouffant hairdo; 'Sis' Buchanan (Mrs Charlie) Mitchell, in hat.

Front row standing: Louise Riley (Mrs. Frank) Holmes; Mrs Colin Currie, dark dress. Seated: Alma "Jo" Ballantyne and her mother, Sarah McJanet (Mrs. George) Ballantyne.

The photo was taken by Mrs. Edna (Malcolm 'Mickey') McDonald. The women are in front of the Beaver Mines Women's Institute hall. The building was built about 1910 and used as a church, a school, the Women's Intitute hall & community hall. Jo Ballantyne Johnson recalled that Miss Tilley was sent out from the Alberta Government, Department of Extension, Edmonton, to teach sewing classes. The ladies each brought a pattern and material to make a simple dress. They had just about enough time to finish the dress by the end of the class.

I remember my mother, Mollie, faithfully attending the Beaver Mines Women's Institute monthly meetings in the 1930s when we lived on the ranch at Beaver Mines. Mollie especially enjoyed the educational component of the Women's Institute program. She looked forward to meetings when a guest speaker from elsewhere, the Women's Institute provincial executive perhaps, visited and spoke on a topic of general interest to farm and ranch women. *Courtesy Adeline Cyr Robbins*

MAPS

In 1918, Dominic Cyr demonstrates perfect form as he builds a haystack on the homestead of him and his wife, Marion Vroom Cyr. It was on NE 33-4-30-W4 near Fish Lake, 12 miles south of Pincher Creek.

Haystacks had to be weatherproof. They had to be built in a certain way to protect the hay from the rain and snow that would fall before the hay was used as fodder for livestock.

The bundle racks are drawn up on either side of the stack. The teams stand quietly while bundles are pitched off one rack and then the other so that the stack is evenly built. An unknown man, perhaps a neighbour or a hired man, helps Dominic by pitching the bundles from the bundle rack onto the stack.

Dominic & his brother, Theodule, opened a butcher shop in Beaver Mines in 1910. Dominic also owned a livery business in Beaver Mines, which is where he met Marion, the aunt of Bessie Ellis. Dominic and Marion's first three children, Alberta, Adeline and Eugene, were under six years old when they lived on the homestead. Esther, Vera and Rita were born when they lived on their farm near Pincher Creek. *Courtesy Adeline Cyr Robbins*

REFERENCES AND SOURCES OF INFORMATION

Bruce, A. Circa 1994. For Nigel and Carolyn. Unpublished manuscript. Personal papers of Heather Bruce Grace, NZ.

Djuff, R. 1999. High on a Windy Hill: The Story of the Prince of Wales Hotel. Rocky Mountain Books, Calgary, AB.

Dormaar, J.F. and Watt, R.A. 2007. Oil City: black gold in Waterton Park. Occasional Paper No. 45 of The Lethbridge Historical Society. City of Lethbridge, Lethbridge, AB.

Drader, E.S. 1963. Letter to Mrs. G.R. Annand, Waterton Park, AB. on 11 November 1963. Personal papers of Bessie Vroom (Annand) Ellis, Victoria, BC.

Early Booms in the Alberta Foothills. Available from the World Wide Web: (http://www.geoexpro.com/geotourism/early_boom)

Getty, I.A.L. 1971. A history of the human settlement at Waterton Lakes National Park, 1800-1937. A research paper prepared fot the National and Historic Parks, National and Historic Parks Branch, Department of Indian Affairs and Northern Development, Ottawa, ON.

Glenbow Archives. Waterton Centennial Oral History Project. Interview of George ("Geordie") Annand, June 16, 1995, by L. Robertson.

Gladstone, GL. 1961. A History of Waterton Lakes National Park, Waterton Park, Alberta. On file with Waterton Lakes National Park Archives.

Goble, F. 2000. The 20 Cent Men. Goble Publishing Limited, Cardston, AB.

Goble, F. 2001. The Waterton School, September 1925 – June 1995. Goble Publishing Limited, Cardston, AB.

Horn, E. Houston, 1995. Angels in the Snow. Esther Horn Publisher, Lethbridge, AB.

Huddlestun, F.A. Circa 1969. A History of the Settlement and Building Up of the Area in S.W. Alberta Bordering Waterton Park on the North From 1889. Privately published.

Huddlestun, G. 1986. Reflections of a Community: Twin Butte Community Hall, Golden Anniversary, 1936-1986. Twin Butte Community Society, Twin Butte, AB.

Lang, R. 1961. Memories of Robert Lang, Pincher Creek, AB. Interview by Bessie M. Annand, Waterton Park, AB. Personal papers of Bessie Vroom Ellis, Victoria, BC.

Library and Archives Canada. 2010. Post offices and postmasters. Available from World Wide Web: (http://www.collectionscanada.gc.ca/databases/post-offices/index-e.html)

Lynch-Staunton, Mrs. C. Circa 1920. A History of the Early Days of Pincher Creek: and of the District and of the Southern Mountains. The Members of the Women's Institute of Alberta, Pincher Creek, AB.

McClelland, E; Oczkowski, V; White, R; Lang, A; Lang, M; Toney, D; Yagos, B; Yagos, S; Paulson, E; Adamson, B. 1970. History of the Beaver Mines Women's Institute: 1920 – 1970. The Beaver Mines Women's Institute, Beaver Mines, AB.

Morrison, C. 2008. Waterton Chronicles: People and their National Park. Goathaunt Publishing, Waterton Park, AB.

Palmer, M.J. and Linebarger, J.J. 1988. Sarah Luela Nielson, Aunt Lu, 4 Feb 1885 – 26 Feb 1965. Unpublished manuscript. On file with Waterton Lakes National Parch Archives.

Pincher Creek and District School Division #29. 1992. Unfolding the Pages. Gorman & Gorman Ltd., Pincher Creek, AB.

Pincher Creek Echo. 1992. 3 Mar.

Pincher Creek Historical Society. 1974. Prairie grass to mountain pass: history of the pioneers of Pincher Creek and district. D.W. Friesen & Sons Ltd., Calgary, AB.

Rodney, W. 1996. "Kootenai" Brown: his life and times 1839-1916. Gray's Publishing Ltd., Sidney, BC.

The Kootenay and Alberta Railway. Available from the World Wide Web: (http://railways-atlas.tapor.ualberta.ca/cocoon/atlas)

The Lethbridge Herald. 1925. 7 May: 5.

The Lethbridge Herald. 1925. 7 August: 10.

The Lethbridge Herald. 1928. 30 August: 4.

The Lethbridge Herald. 1944. 23 June: 9.

The Lethbridge Herald. 1947. 11 December: 47.

The Lethbridge Herald. 1948. 24 July: 6.

The Lethbridge Herald. 1951. 21 August. 3.

Western Land Grants. 1870-1930 (online). Legal land description. Available from World Wide Web: (http://collectionscanada.gc.ca/databases/western-land-grants)

Wuth, F. 2008. The History That Almost Wasn't: Chronicales of Pincher Creek's Ill-Fated Rail Industry. The Pincher Creek and District Historical Society, Pincher Creek, AB.

INDEX

ABOUT THE AUTHOR

The VROOMS of the FOOTHILLS, Volume 3: When the Work's All Done This Fall is the third volume in the social history series by Bessie Vroom Ellis. The first two volumes are: *The VROOMS of the FOOTHILLS: Adventures of My Childhood*, Trafford, 2006; and The VROOMS of the FOOTHILLS: *Cowboys & Homesteaders*, Trafford, 2008.

The VROOMS of the FOOTHILLS, Volume 3: When the Work's All Done This Fall uses over 270 pictures to tell of the many ways that people made a living in western Canada in the late 19th to mid-20th centuries. Families are also shown having fun in a variety of ways.

The author attended one-room country schools for her elementary grades, riding on horseback and making a round trip of nearly nine miles each day. She graduated from Pincher Creek High School and attended Calgary Normal School. When she first taught in Waterton Park in 1947-1948 Ms. Ellis (nee Vroom) met and married local resident George "Geordie" Annand Jr. They raised a family of four children, Edi-May (Smithies), Evelyn (Lailey), David and James Annand.

During her more than 20 years in Waterton Park, the author honed her writing skills. She wrote feature articles and a thrice-weekly column, Wonderful Waterton, for *The Lethbridge Herald.* As well, Ms. Ellis contributed news items to three other newspapers— two in Calgary and one in Montana—and to CJOC Radio and CJLH-TV in Lethbridge, AB. She was active in the Girl Guides of Canada and in the Anglican Church of Canada.

After 15 years the author returned to her teaching career, updating her qualifications through night extension classes, Summer School and day classes. She was awarded a Bachelor of Education degree by the University of Lethbridge and a Master of Education degree by University of Alberta, and then taught in Lethbridge, AB. After her remarriage in 1975 Ms. Ellis moved to Regina, SK, teaching there for another 15 years for a total of over 29 years of service in the teaching profession. In Regina she earned a post-graduate Diploma in Educational Administration from the University of Regina.

During her years in Regina the author travelled extensively. She was active in politics running for office herself and then working to promote the election of more women at the provincial and federal levels. In the early 1980s the Saskatchewan New Democratic Women (SNDW) established the Bessie Ellis Fund to assist women running for nomination.

In 1992 Bessie was awarded the Commemorative Medal for the 125th Anniversary of the Confederation Canada, 1867 – 1992, "in recognition of significant contribution to compatriots, community and to Canada." Upon retirement Bessie returned to her writing.